Better Homes and Gardens®

Low-Fat
COOKING

Our seal assures you that every recipe in *Low-Fat Cooking*
has been tested in the Better Homes and Gardens® Test Kitchen.
This means that each recipe is practical and reliable, and
meets our high standards of taste appeal.

BETTER HOMES AND GARDENS® BOOKS
Editor: Gerald M. Knox
Art Director: Ernest Shelton
Managing Editor: David A. Kirchner
Copy and Production Editors: Marsha Jahns, Mary Helen Schiltz,
    Carl Voss, David A. Walsh

Food and Nutrition Editor: Nancy Byal
Department Head—Cook Books: Sharyl Heiken
Associate Department Heads: Sandra Granseth,
    Rosemary C. Hutchinson, Elizabeth Woolever
Senior Food Editors: Julia Malloy, Marcia Stanley, Joyce Trollope
Associate Food Editors: Barbara Atkins, Linda Foley, Linda Henry,
    Lynn Hoppe, Jill Johnson, Mary Jo Plutt, Maureen Powers
Recipe Development Editor: Marion Viall
Test Kitchen Director: Sharon Stilwell
Test Kitchen Photo Studio Director: Janet Pittman
Test Kitchen Home Economists: Jean Brekke, Kay Cargill,
    Marilyn Cornelius, Jennifer Darling, Maryellyn Krantz,
    Lynelle Munn, Dianna Nolin, Marge Steenson, Cynthia Volcko

Associate Art Directors: Linda Ford Vermie, Neoma Alt West,
    Randall Yontz
Assistant Art Directors: Lynda Haupert, Harijs Priekulis,
    Tom Wegner
Senior Graphic Designers: Mike Eagleton, Lyne Neymeyer,
    Stan Sams
Graphic Designers: Mike Burns, Sally Cooper,
    Darla Whipple-Frain, Brian Wignall

Vice President, Editorial Director: Doris Eby
Executive Director, Editorial Services: Duane L. Gregg

Senior Vice President, General Manager: Fred Stines
Director of Publishing: Robert B. Nelson
Vice President, Retail Marketing: Jamie Martin
Vice President, Direct Marketing: Arthur Heydendael

LOW-FAT COOKING
Editor: Linda Foley
Copy and Production Editor: Marsha Jahns
Graphic Designer: Stan Sams
Electronic Text Processor: Joyce Wasson
Contributing Photographer: Mike Dieter
Food Stylist: Janet Pittman
Contributing Illustrator: Tom Rosborough

On the front cover: Tamale Lentil Soup
(see recipe, page 46)

It's amazing how accustomed we become to high-fat foods without a second thought. In my recipe research, for example, I discovered that a simple tuna casserole, my childhood favorite, was loaded with fat. With the help of the Test Kitchen I eliminated a big chunk of fat from this recipe. From now on, I'm sticking with the Tuna-Mac Casserole on page 22. It's every bit as rich and creamy as the one Mom made, minus about half the fat!

I also found that trimming fat from recipes, while preserving great taste, was really quite easy. Throughout the book you'll find recipes using low-fat cooking techniques. Beginning on page 84, we show you these tricks so you can apply them to your own recipes. Maybe all that's needed is to substitute low-fat yogurt for sour cream, as in the Beef Stroganoff on page 87. Or, try using less oil in salad dressings, as in the Vinaigrette Dressing on page 88.

Building entire meals low in fat is another challenge I've tried to meet in this book. Many recipes are photographed with other low-fat foods so you'll know how to round out your meals. Another bonus is the Fat and Cholesterol Chart on page 90, which furnishes fat and cholesterol counts of everyday foods. As I did, you may find a few eye-openers.

This cook book is proof positive that low-fat eating is practically painless! I hope the recipes, hints, and information are just the start of healthier, more enjoyable eating for you.

Linda Foley

FAT FACTS 6

MAIN DISHES 8

SIDE DISHES 50

Fat Facts

It's not necessary to know all the mechanical workings of a car to drive one. So it follows that you don't have to be a biochemist to get the hang of low-fat eating. What follows is a trimmed down, no-nonsense guide that explains what fats are and how they affect you. It's designed to make low-fat eating easier for you to swallow!

What's What with Fats

Fats appear as solids, liquids, or a combination of these in an astounding variety of foods. Basically, fats fall into two categories: saturated and unsaturated fats.
● Saturated fats are almost always solid when at room temperature. The main source usually is animal fat. Meats, chicken fat, meat fats such as lard and suet, dairy products such as butter and cream, and coconut oil all harbor saturated fats.
● Unsaturated fats are soft or liquid at room temperature. Plants provide the source for most unsaturated fat. Vegetable oils such as corn, safflower, and soybean are prime examples. We can categorize unsaturated fats even further. You get monounsaturated fats in olives, olive oil, peanut butter, avocados, and cashews. Polyunsaturated fats are found in almonds, corn oil, fish, and margarine made from vegetable oil.

What Can Fats Do FOR You?

In a word, fat is energy—9 calories in every gram. It's a powerpack, because carbohydrates and proteins carry only half as much. It's no wonder that a little fat goes such a long way!

The key to getting the best of fat lies in being very selective. Polyunsaturated fats (vegetable oils) get the best marks for nutrient value. They carry vitamins A, D, E, and K through your system. In the process, polyunsaturates also generate fatty acids, such as linoleic acid, that are necessary to life.

The Big C—Cholesterol

First, a few surprises. Cholesterol, though fatlike, is technically not a fat. It's actually a nutrient manufactured in generous amounts by your liver. Cholesterol helps produce vitamin D, blankets nerve fibers, and lends durability to cell walls.

In addition to the cholesterol your body makes, saturated fats and cholesterol in many foods add to the supply. However, the effect this has on your health is being studied. If you're watching cholesterol, cut down on meats (especially organ meats), animal fat, dairy products, egg yolks, shrimp, and sardines.

What's the Bottom Line?

If you're in a fog about how much fat and cholesterol to eat, let's clear the air. Public health organizations offer a three-point prescription:
  1) Fats should comprise just one-third (30 to 35%) of total daily calories.
  2) No more than one-third of fat calories should be in the form of saturated fat.
  3) Your diet should contain no more than 300 milligrams of cholesterol daily.

Recipe Facts and Figures

Enter our computer; it's a storehouse of information on nutrients, calories, and Recommended Daily Allowance percentages from Agriculture Handbook No. 456 by the U.S. Department of Agriculture. The chart at the end of each chapter translates computerese into easy-to-read facts on every recipe.

In the process, we assumed the following:
● Garnishes and optional ingredients were omitted from the nutrition analysis.
● Statistics on meat in recipes were based on cooked lean meat trimmed of fat.
● Ingredients with a weight range (a 2½- to 3-pound chicken, for example) were analyzed at the lesser weight.
● Where you find two ingredient options to pick from, the first was used in the nutrition rundown.

Reducing Fat in Chicken Enchiladas

Bypass the Dark Meat
We wanted to make a rich-tasting enchilada filling that was high in flavor, not fat. Because the light meat of poultry is leaner than the dark meat, we stuffed the tortillas with a mixture that uses the breast of chicken or turkey as its base. And we removed the skin from the poultry for even more fat savings.

Don't Fry the Tortillas
Put away the frypan! You can skip the fat and mess of frying the tortillas in oil simply by warming them in the oven. Chalk up another fat-sparing bonus by using corn tortillas, which have less fat than flour tortillas.

Avoid High-Fat Garnishes
Garnishes aren't just for looks—they can be part of a meal, too. That's why we adorned the plate with juicy tomato wedges instead of high-fat avocado slices. We also replaced sour cream and ripe olives with plain low-fat yogurt and sliced green onion.

Chicken Enchiladas
(see recipe, page 14)

Name your favorite main dish. Feeling guilty about your choice? Unfortunately, many popular entrées flaunt fat. But wait! With a few smart recipe alterations, like slipping in lean protein foods and using nearly fat-free cooking methods, voilà! Traditional favorites become low-fat fare — deliciously.

Savor our hearty stews, stuffed chops, and roasts (with gravy, yet). Enjoy them all, now that we've reduced the fat but not the fun.

Poultry

Poultry is a real blessing for low-fat fanciers. But first you need to know how to capitalize on the lean qualities of chicken and turkey.

An easy way to trim down poultry is by removing all of the skin, as well as those cleverly hidden pockets of fat just beneath the skin. Cut up the bird before skinning, and have a pair of kitchen scissors nearby to help cut away any stubborn skin, especially on the wings.

Once the skin is gone, look closely at the type of meat. The light meat is leaner than the dark meat, so always make that your first choice.

With poultry, biggest is not necessarily best. Larger, older birds such as roasters and capons are fattier than smaller, younger chickens and turkeys.

Also, check out your supermarket meat case for some exciting new poultry-based products. Case in point: turkey bologna. With almost half of the fat gone, one serving weighs in at 100 calories less than beef or pork bologna.

Chicken-Vegetable Stew

12 grams fat/serving

A perfect cold weather warmer!

Nonstick spray coating
12 chicken thighs, skinned (about 3 pounds total)
3½ cups water
1 cup chopped onion
1 clove garlic, minced
1 bay leaf
1 tablespoon instant chicken bouillon granules
1 teaspoon dried thyme, crushed
¼ teaspoon pepper
2 medium parsnips, peeled and cubed
1 cup fresh *or* frozen brussels sprouts, halved
1 cup loose-pack frozen mixed vegetables
⅓ cup cornstarch
⅓ cup cold water
Cornmeal Biscuit Wedges

● Spray a Dutch oven with nonstick coating. Brown chicken in the kettle for 10 minutes. Add 3½ cups water, onion, garlic, bay leaf, bouillon, thyme, and pepper. Bring to boiling; reduce heat. Cover and simmer for 15 minutes.

● Stir in parsnips, brussels sprouts, and mixed vegetables. Return to boiling; reduce heat. Cover and simmer for 10 to 15 minutes or just until vegetables are tender. Combine ⅓ cup water and cornstarch. Add to kettle. Cook and stir till thickened and bubbly, then cook and stir 2 minutes more. Top with baked Cornmeal Biscuit Wedges. Makes 6 servings.

Cornmeal Biscuit Wedges: Stir together ¾ cup all-purpose *flour,* ¼ cup yellow *cornmeal,* 1 tablespoon finely snipped *parsley,* 2 teaspoons *baking powder,* and 1 teaspoon *sugar.* Cut in ¼ cup *margarine* till mixture resembles coarse crumbs. Make a well in the center, then add ¼ cup *skim milk.* Stir just till dough clings together. Knead gently on a lightly floured surface for 10 to 12 strokes. Roll or pat dough into a 6- or 7-inch circle; cut into six wedges. Bake on an ungreased baking sheet in a 450° oven for 8 to 10 minutes or till golden. Serve warm.

Chicken Couscous

5 grams fat/serving

This North African favorite gets its name from the grain.

Nonstick spray coating
1 2½- to 3-pound broiler-fryer chicken, cut up and skinned
2 medium onions, coarsely chopped
1 clove garlic, minced
1 15-ounce can garbanzo beans, drained and rinsed
1 10½-ounce can tomato puree
1 7½-ounce can tomatoes, cut up
½ cup raisins
½ cup water
2 bay leaves
6 inches stick cinnamon
1½ teaspoons chili powder
½ teaspoon ground ginger
½ teaspoon ground cumin
4 cups desired fresh vegetables*
1 cup quick-cooking couscous

● Spray a Dutch oven with nonstick coating. Brown chicken pieces on one side for 7 minutes. Turn chicken, then add onion and garlic. Cook about 8 minutes more or till chicken is brown and onion is tender. Stir in garbanzo beans, tomato puree, *undrained* tomatoes, raisins, water, bay leaves, cinnamon, chili powder, ginger, and cumin. Stir in vegetables. Bring to boiling; reduce heat. Cover and simmer about 30 minutes or till chicken and vegetables are tender. Discard bay leaves and cinnamon.

● Meanwhile, stir couscous into 1 cup *boiling water.* Remove from the heat, then let stand for 3 to 4 minutes or just till liquid is absorbed. To serve, mound couscous and chicken mixture on a serving platter. Makes 6 servings.

*For vegetables, choose any of the following: carrots, cut into ¼-inch slices; celery, cut into 1-inch pieces; zucchini, halved lengthwise and cut into ½-inch slices; green pepper, cut into bite-size pieces; turnip, peeled and cut into ¼-inch cubes; and chopped cabbage.

Curry Country Chicken

4 grams fat/serving

Nonstick spray coating
1 2½- to 3-pound broiler-fryer chicken, cut up and skinned
½ cup chopped onion
½ cup chopped green pepper
1 clove garlic, minced
1 16-ounce can tomatoes, cut up
¼ cup dried currants *or* raisins
¼ cup snipped parsley
2 teaspoons curry powder
½ teaspoon ground mace *or* nutmeg
⅛ teaspoon pepper
2 tablespoons cold water
1 tablespoon cornstarch
3 cups hot cooked rice

● Spray a large skillet with nonstick coating. Brown chicken in the skillet for 15 minutes, turning once. Add onion, green pepper, and garlic. Stir in *undrained* tomatoes, currants or raisins, parsley, curry powder, mace or nutmeg, and pepper. Bring to boiling; reduce heat. Simmer, uncovered, about 30 minutes or till chicken is tender.

● Remove chicken; keep warm. Skim excess fat from sauce, if necessary. Combine water and cornstarch; stir into sauce. Cook and stir till thickened and bubbly, then cook and stir 2 minutes more. Serve chicken and sauce over rice. Makes 6 servings.

Chicken Couscous

Barbecued Oven-Fried Chicken

4 grams fat/serving

1 2½- to 3-pound broiler-fryer
    chicken, cut up and
    skinned
½ cup crushed wheat wafers
    (about 35 crackers)
1 teaspoon chili powder
½ teaspoon garlic powder
¼ teaspoon dry mustard
¼ teaspoon celery seed
⅛ teaspoon ground red pepper
¼ cup barbecue sauce

● Rinse chicken, then pat dry with paper towels. Stir together crushed wafers and seasonings. Brush each chicken piece with barbecue sauce; roll in crumb mixture to coat.

● Arrange chicken, bone side down and so pieces don't touch, in a shallow baking pan. Sprinkle with any remaining crumb mixture. Bake in a 375° oven about 50 minutes or till chicken is tender and coating is crisp. *Do not* turn. Makes 6 servings.

Individual Bread Bowls

4 grams fat/serving

Take a peek at the opposite page to master these edible soup bowls.

1 to 1½ cups all-purpose flour
1 package active dry yeast
¾ cup skim milk
1 tablespoon margarine
1 tablespoon honey
¾ cup rye flour
    Nonstick spray coating
1 slightly beaten egg white
1 tablespoon water

● Combine *1 cup* all-purpose flour and yeast. Heat milk, margarine, and honey just till warm (115° to 120°) and margarine almost melts; add to flour mixture. Beat with an electric mixer on low speed for 30 seconds. Beat 3 minutes on high speed. Stir in rye flour and as much remaining all-purpose flour as you can.

● Turn dough onto a lightly floured surface, then knead in enough remaining flour to make a moderately stiff dough that is smooth and elastic (6 to 8 minutes total). Place in a greased bowl, then turn to grease surface. Cover; let rise in a warm place till double (about 1 hour). Punch down. Cover and set aside *one-third* of the dough. Divide remaining dough into four portions. Shape each into a smooth ball. Cover; let rest 10 minutes.

● Roll each ball of dough into a 7-inch circle. Spray four inverted 10-ounce custard cups with nonstick coating, then fit dough over custard cups. Trim dough at edge of dish. Place on a baking sheet sprayed with nonstick coating.

● Bake the bread bowls in a 375° oven for 5 minutes. Meanwhile, on a floured surface roll reserved dough into a 12x9-inch rectangle. Cut into desired shapes about 2 inches in diameter. Combine egg white and water. Brush bowls with egg white mixture. Press cutouts onto edge of each bowl; brush with egg white mixture. Continue baking for 5 to 7 minutes or till almost done (if dough puffs up, press down with a pot holder). Remove bread from custard cups. Place bread right side up on a baking sheet. Brush with egg white mixture. Continue baking about 10 minutes more or till brown, covering edges with foil the last 5 minutes; cool. Makes 4 servings.

Chicken Chowder in Bread Bowls

A champion chowder, with or without the bread bowls.

Individual Bread Bowls
  (see recipe, opposite page)
2 whole medium chicken
    breasts, skinned and
    boned
1 cup water
1 medium onion, chopped
1 medium carrot, shredded
1 clove garlic, minced
2 teaspoons instant chicken
    bouillon granules
¼ teaspoon ground red pepper
1 medium potato, peeled and
    cut up
1 12-ounce can (1½ cups)
    evaporated skimmed milk
1 tablespoon cornstarch
2 tablespoons snipped chives

● Prepare and bake Individual Bread Bowls; cool. In a saucepan combine chicken, water, onion, carrot, garlic, bouillon granules, and pepper. Bring to boiling; reduce heat. Cover and simmer for 10 minutes. Stir in potato, then cover and simmer about 15 minutes more or till chicken and potato are tender. Remove chicken. When cool enough to handle, cut into bite-size pieces; return to saucepan. Mash potato slightly.

● Combine milk and cornstarch; add to saucepan. Cook and stir till thickened and bubbly, then cook and stir 2 minutes more. Serve in bread bowls; sprinkle with chives. Makes 4 servings.

Glazing the bread bowls
After taking the partially baked bread bowls out of the oven, use a narrow metal spatula to remove the bread from the inverted custard cups.

Use a pastry brush to coat the insides and edges of the bowls with the egg white mixture. As the bread bowls finish baking, the egg white forms a hard glossy layer, making the bowls sturdy enough to hold the hot chowder.

Chicken Enchiladas

10 grams fat/serving

Olé! Stuff tortillas with creamy chicken filling, top with spicy sauce and cheese, and enjoy.

1 15-ounce can tomato sauce
1 4-ounce can diced green
    chili peppers, rinsed and
    drained
2 teaspoons sugar
½ teaspoon ground coriander
    Nonstick spray coating
¼ cup finely chopped onion
2 ounces Neufchâtel cheese,
    softened
¼ cup skim milk
2 cups finely chopped cooked
    chicken *or* turkey
2 tablespoons snipped parsley
12 6-inch corn tortillas
⅓ cup shredded Monterey
    Jack cheese (1½ ounces)

● For sauce, combine tomato sauce, green chili peppers, sugar, and coriander. Set aside.

● Spray a saucepan with nonstick coating. Cook onion in the saucepan till tender. Stir in Neufchâtel cheese and milk till smooth. Stir in chicken or turkey and parsley. Wrap tortillas in foil and heat in a 350° oven about 10 minutes or till warm. Spoon chicken mixture on tortillas, then roll up.

● Spray a 12x7½x2-inch baking dish with nonstick coating. Place tortillas, seam side down, in the dish. Cover with foil. Bake in a 350° oven for 20 to 25 minutes or till heated through. Pour sauce over tortillas, then sprinkle with Monterey Jack cheese. Return to the oven; bake, uncovered, for 5 to 7 minutes more or till sauce is hot and cheese melts. Makes 6 servings.

Chicken Tetrazzini

6 grams fat/serving

Named for the Italian opera star Luisa Tetrazzini, who was known for her outstanding voice and love of pasta.

6 ounces spaghetti, broken
    into 3- to 4-inch lengths
1 cup water
2 teaspoons instant chicken
    bouillon granules
3 whole medium chicken
    breasts, skinned and
    halved lengthwise
1½ cups sliced fresh
    mushrooms
½ cup coarsely chopped green
    pepper
1⅔ cups skim milk
3 tablespoons cornstarch
    Dash salt
    Dash pepper
¼ cup grated Parmesan cheese
3 tablespoons dry sherry
2 tablespoons sliced almonds,
    toasted

● Cook spaghetti according to package directions; drain. Meanwhile, in a large skillet combine water and bouillon granules. Bring to boiling. Add chicken. Return to boiling; reduce heat. Cover and simmer for 20 to 25 minutes or till tender. Remove chicken; cool. Remove meat from bones, then discard bones. Cut chicken into bite-size pieces; set aside. Skim fat from cooking liquid. Strain liquid, reserving 1 cup.

● In the same skillet combine the reserved liquid, mushrooms, and green pepper. Bring to boiling; reduce heat. Cover and simmer about 5 minutes or till tender. Combine milk, cornstarch, salt, and pepper; add to skillet. Cook and stir till thickened and bubbly, then cook and stir 2 minutes more. Stir in *half* of the cheese and the sherry, then fold in chicken and spaghetti.

● Place mixture in a 12x7½x2-inch baking dish. Sprinkle with remaining cheese and almonds. Bake in a 400° oven for 10 to 15 minutes or till heated through. Makes 6 servings.

Almond Chicken à l'Orange

A 6-ounce package of frozen pea pods can pinch-hit for fresh.

2 whole medium chicken breasts, skinned and boned
2 tablespoons soy sauce
2 teaspoons cornstarch
1 teaspoon finely shredded orange peel
2 tablespoons orange juice
2 tablespoons dry sherry
Nonstick spray coating
1 teaspoon grated gingerroot
2 cups fresh pea pods
4 medium green onions, sliced into 1-inch pieces
1 11-ounce can mandarin orange sections, drained
½ cup sliced almonds, toasted
2 cups hot cooked rice

● Cut chicken into bite-size pieces. Combine soy sauce and cornstarch. Stir in orange peel, juice, and sherry; set aside.

● Spray a wok or large skillet with nonstick coating. Stir-fry gingerroot in the wok for 15 seconds. Add pea pods and onions; stir-fry about 2 minutes or till crisp-tender. Remove from wok. Add half of the chicken to wok; stir-fry for 2 minutes. Remove from wok. Stir-fry remaining chicken for 2 minutes. Return all chicken to wok. Push meat from center of wok.

● Stir soy sauce mixture and add to wok. Cook and stir till thickened and bubbly, then cook and stir 2 minutes more. Return vegetables to wok, then stir in oranges. Cover and cook about 1 minute more or till hot. Add almonds. Serve immediately with rice. Makes 4 servings.

Learn from Labels

Get into the habit of reading package labels. They'll tell you not only how much but also what type of fat is in the food.

When reading a product label, remember that the first ingredients listed are present in the greatest quantity. So, if fat(s) is mentioned early in the list, you can bet the food is high in fat. If fat(s) appears near the end, however, you'll know the food is relatively low in fat.

Another factor to consider is the type of fat in a product. Keep in mind that the vegetable oils highest in unsaturated fats are safflower, walnut, corn, sunflower, soybean, wheat germ, and cottonseed. Common monounsaturated fats are olive and peanut oil; saturated fats include palm oil and coconut oil.

Sometimes you'll see "hydrogenated fat" or "partially hydrogenated fat" on the label. This simply means hydrogen was added to the fat. Though this makes the fat slower to spoil, it also makes it more saturated.

If the label doesn't list what you want to know, write to the manufacturer.

Broiled Turkey with
Raspberry Sauce

Broiled Turkey with Raspberry Sauce

A versatile sauce! We also loved it with the chocolate-nutmeg dessert on page 67.

6 boneless turkey breast
tenderloin steaks (about
1½ pounds total)
1 tablespoon lemon juice
1 tablespoon water
2 teaspoons soy sauce
1 10-ounce package frozen
red raspberries, thawed
2 tablespoons dry white wine
1 tablespoon orange liqueur
or orange juice
2 teaspoons cornstarch
Fresh raspberries (optional)

● Rinse turkey, then pat dry with paper towels. Place on a rack in an unheated broiler pan. Combine lemon juice, water, and soy sauce. Brush turkey with lemon mixture. Broil 5 inches from the heat for 6 minutes. Turn and broil about 6 minutes more or till tender, brushing occasionally with lemon mixture.

● Meanwhile, place thawed raspberries in a blender container or food processor bowl. Cover and blend till smooth. Sieve; discard seeds. In a saucepan combine wine, orange liqueur or orange juice, and cornstarch. Add sieved raspberries. Cook and stir till thickened and bubbly, then cook and stir 2 minutes more. Serve sauce with turkey. Garnish with fresh berries, if desired. Makes 6 servings.

Curried Turkey Salad

Reduced-calorie mayonnaise saves you more than half the fat of regular mayonnaise.

⅓ cup plain low-fat yogurt
¼ cup reduced-calorie
mayonnaise
1 tablespoon skim milk
1 teaspoon curry powder
¼ teaspoon salt
⅛ teaspoon pepper
3 cups chopped cooked
turkey *or* chicken breast
1 cup halved and seeded
grapes
½ cup chopped water
chestnuts
½ cup chopped green pepper
6 lettuce leaves

● In a mixing bowl combine yogurt, mayonnaise, milk, curry powder, salt, and pepper; mix well. Fold in turkey or chicken, grapes, water chestnuts, and green pepper. Cover and chill. Serve on lettuce leaves. Makes 6 servings.

Fish and Seafood

Fish must swim, so maybe that accounts for their (mostly) wonderful leanness! The fat tally for most fish is refreshingly low, and you have plenty of varieties to choose from. Cod, haddock, halibut, flounder, sole, red snapper, and orange roughie all qualify for delicious low-fat dining.

Take note, however, that fish skin is similar to poultry skin. It contains oils that cook into the flesh if not removed. So when buying fresh or frozen fish, ask to have the skin removed or choose skinless fillets.

Other fish are oily throughout the meat, so choose them less frequently.

Sardines, salmon, lake trout, and mackerel fall into this category. Tuna also harbors oil in its flesh, but if you opt for the canned water-pack type, you'll be better off.

Shellfish are a mixed blessing. Though shrimp is high in cholesterol, for example, it's unmistakably low in fat.

Spicy Asparagus Fish Rolls

8 grams fat/serving

Some like it hot! The green chili peppers with the canned tomatoes pack a punch.

4 fresh *or* frozen flounder
　　or other fish fillets
　　(about 1 pound total)
¾ pound fresh asparagus
　　or one 10-ounce package
　　frozen asparagus spears
　　Nonstick spray coating
1½ teaspoons margarine,
　　melted
¼ cup finely chopped onion
1½ teaspoons margarine
1½ teaspoons cornstarch
½ teaspoon dried basil,
　　crushed
1 10-ounce can tomatoes and
　　green chili peppers
½ cup shredded Monterey
　　Jack cheese (2 ounces)

● Thaw fish, if frozen. Cut fresh asparagus into 6-inch lengths. Cook fresh asparagus, covered, in a small amount of boiling water for 8 to 10 minutes or till crisp-tender. (Or, cook frozen asparagus according to package directions.) Drain.

● Place *three or four* asparagus spears crosswise on *each* fillet, then roll up fillets. Place, seam side down, in four individual baking dishes sprayed with nonstick coating. Brush fish with 1½ teaspoons melted margarine. Bake, uncovered, in a 350° oven about 20 minutes or until fish is nearly done. Drain excess liquid from dishes.

● For sauce, cook onion in 1½ teaspoons margarine till tender. Stir in cornstarch and basil. Add tomatoes and green chili peppers. Cook and stir till thickened and bubbly, then cook and stir 2 minutes more. Pour over fish rolls. Sprinkle with cheese. Bake, uncovered, for 3 to 5 minutes more or until fish flakes easily with a fork. Makes 4 servings.

Baked Stuffed Whitefish

We left the skin (which contains oils) on the fish in order to stuff it, but kept it lean with a slim filling and a low-fat cooking method.

1   2½- to 3-pound fresh *or* frozen dressed whitefish *or* other fish
    Nonstick spray coating
1   small carrot, shredded
¼   cup finely chopped onion
¼   cup finely chopped green pepper
1   clove garlic, minced
2   tablespoons snipped parsley
½   teaspoon dried basil, crushed
¼   teaspoon finely shredded lemon peel
¼   teaspoon salt
    Dash pepper
3   cups dry whole wheat *or* rye bread cubes (4 slices)
2   teaspoons lemon juice
¼   to ⅓ cup chicken broth
1   teaspoon cooking oil

● Thaw fish, if frozen; pat dry with paper towels. Spray a shallow baking pan with nonstick coating. Place fish in the pan.

● For stuffing, spray a saucepan with nonstick coating. Cook carrot, onion, green pepper, and garlic in the saucepan till tender. Remove from heat. Stir in parsley, basil, lemon peel, salt, and pepper. Add bread cubes; toss. Drizzle with lemon juice, then add enough chicken broth to moisten. Toss lightly.

● Fill fish cavity loosely with stuffing. Brush skin of fish with oil. Cover loosely with foil. Bake in a 350° oven for 45 to 60 minutes or until fish flakes easily with a fork. Use two large spatulas to lift fish to a serving platter. Makes 5 servings.

Halibut Steaks with Sherry Sauce

You can substitute 1-inch-thick salmon steaks for the halibut.

2   pounds fresh *or* frozen halibut steaks, cut 1 inch thick
    Nonstick spray coating
1   tablespoon margarine, melted
¼   cup sliced green onion
1   clove garlic, minced
½   cup water
½   teaspoon instant chicken bouillon granules
1   tablespoon all-purpose flour
¼   cup plain low-fat yogurt
1   2½-ounce jar sliced mushrooms, drained
1   tablespoon dry sherry
    Paprika

● Thaw fish, if frozen. Cut fish into six portions. Spray the rack of an unheated broiler pan with nonstick coating. Place fish on the rack. Brush with *half* of the melted margarine, then sprinkle lightly with salt and pepper.

● Broil fish 4 inches from the heat for 5 minutes; turn. Brush with remaining melted margarine. Broil 5 to 8 minutes more or till fish flakes easily with a fork.

● Meanwhile, spray a saucepan with nonstick coating. Cook onion and garlic in the saucepan till tender. Add water and bouillon granules. Stir flour into yogurt; add to saucepan. Cook and stir till thickened and bubbly, then cook and stir 1 minute more. Stir in mushrooms and sherry; heat through. Serve over fish. Sprinkle with paprika. Makes 6 servings.

Sole en Papillote

Paper cookery at its best—elegant, easy, and low-fat.

1 to 1¼ pounds fresh *or*
   frozen sole *or* other
   fish fillets
¼ cup dry vermouth
   Nonstick spray coating
2 cups sliced fresh
   mushrooms
2 green onions, sliced
4 15x12-inch pieces
   parchment paper
1 tablespoon margarine,
   melted
   Pepper
4 lemon slices

● Thaw fish, if frozen. Cut into four pieces. Place fish in a shallow dish, then add vermouth. Cover and marinate in the refrigerator for 1 hour. Spray a skillet with nonstick coating. Cook mushrooms and onions in the skillet till tender.

● Remove fish from vermouth. Add vermouth to mushroom mixture. Cook mixture over medium heat till liquid evaporates. Meanwhile, fold each piece of parchment paper in half lengthwise, then cut a half-heart shape on the folded edge.

● To assemble, open one parchment heart and brush *half* of it with some melted margarine. Place one fish portion on the brushed half of heart, cutting fillet as necessary to fit. Top with ¼ of the mushroom mixture, then sprinkle with pepper. Place lemon slice on the fillet. Fold paper and seal the package, as shown on the opposite page, making four bundles total. Place bundles on a baking sheet.

● Bake in a 450° oven about 10 minutes or until paper puffs up. *Or,* carefully unwrap paper and test with a fork for doneness. Slit bundles; transfer to serving plates. Makes 4 servings.

Nonstick Spray Coating

A slick way to save fat, cholesterol, and calories during cooking is to use nonstick spray coating.

Several brands of nonstick spray coating are now available, and each product description is a little different. On your grocer's shelf you may find this nonstick cooking product marked as "natural vegetable coating," "vegetable or corn oil cooking spray," or simply "cooking spray."

Regardless of the description, all of the sprays contain vegetable oil. Read the label to discover additional ingredients.

Basically, the fat-saving concept is to eliminate the need for cooking oil. When you spray a small amount of nonstick coating onto a skillet or baking dish, it forms a very thin film that prevents food from sticking.

Be sure to read and follow the directions before using any of these products.

1 Folding the Sole en Papillote

After arranging the fish, mushroom mixture, and lemon slice on half of a section of parchment paper, seal the package by carefully folding the edges together in a double fold. Fold only a small section of the parchment paper at a time to ensure a tight seal. This allows the fish to steam in the enclosed package.

You also can use brown paper as a suitable alternative to parchment paper. Look for both kinds of paper at kitchen shops or in the paper section of your grocery store.

2 Serving the fish bundles

During baking, the parchment paper will puff up and become light brown. This is a good sign that the fish is done.

Just before serving, slit open the top of each packet with a small scissors or sharp knife and let the steam escape. Place each packet on a serving plate. That way diners can enjoy the fun of opening their own packets by tearing gently at the slits.

Citrus Salmon Steaks

12 grams fat/serving

Heat up the coals and get out the grill basket for this one.

1 pound fresh *or* frozen
  salmon *or* halibut steaks,
  cut 1 inch thick
1 teaspoon finely shredded
  orange peel
½ cup orange juice
1 tablespoon snipped parsley
1 teaspoon cooking oil
½ teaspoon dried dillweed
⅛ teaspoon salt
⅛ teaspoon pepper
  Nonstick spray coating
4 thin orange slices (optional)

● Thaw fish, if frozen. Cut fish into four portions. Place in a shallow baking dish. For marinade, combine orange peel, juice, parsley, oil, dillweed, salt, and pepper; pour over fish. Cover and marinate in the refrigerator for 45 minutes, turning once. Remove fish, reserving marinade.

● Spray a wire grill basket with nonstick coating, then place fish in the basket. Grill over *medium-hot* coals for 5 to 8 minutes or till lightly browned. Brush with marinade, then turn basket. Grill for 5 to 8 minutes more or till fish flakes easily when tested with a fork, brushing often with marinade. Garnish with orange slices, if desired. Makes 4 servings.

Tuna-Mac Casserole

3 grams fat/serving

An old family favorite gets a fat-trimming face-lift.

6 ounces elbow macaroni
  (1½ cups)
½ cup chopped celery
½ cup chopped carrot
¼ cup chopped onion
1 10¾-ounce can condensed
  cream of celery soup
¾ cup skim milk
¼ teaspoon salt (optional)
2 6-ounce cans tuna, drained
  and flaked (water pack)
1 cup frozen peas, thawed
1 tablespoon grated
  Parmesan cheese

● Cook macaroni, celery, carrot, and onion in a large amount of boiling water for 8 to 10 minutes or till pasta is tender; drain. Stir in soup, milk, and salt, if desired. Fold in tuna and peas.

● Place in a 2-quart casserole. Cover and bake in a 375° oven for 25 minutes. Stir, then sprinkle with cheese. Cover and bake about 5 minutes more or till heated through. Makes 6 servings.

Low-Fat Cooking Tips

Cutting fat and cholesterol in your everyday cooking is probably easier than you think. Here are a few ways to do just that.

● Broil or roast meats and poultry to allow the fat to drip away from the food.

● Skip the butter or margarine called for in the package directions for cooking rice.

● When a recipe calls for whole milk, light or heavy cream, or evaporated milk, remember that evaporated skim milk provides almost the same richness with less than 1 gram of fat per ½ cup.

● Cut fat and calories by sautéing foods in a minimum of cooking oil or by using nonstick spray coating or nonstick pans.

● Make a great-tasting, low-fat mayonnaise by mixing equal parts plain low-fat yogurt and reduced-calorie mayonnaise.

● Cut fat by more than 75 percent by substituting plain low-fat yogurt for dairy sour cream.

Cioppino-Style Stew

1 gram fat/serving

A terrific tomato-based stew, pronounced chuh-PEE-no, with a hearty hodgepodge of fish, clams, vegetables, and seasonings.

¾ pound fresh *or* frozen fish fillets
1 medium green pepper, cut into ½-inch pieces
½ cup finely chopped onion
2 tablespoons water
1 clove garlic, minced
1 16-ounce can tomatoes, cut up
1 8-ounce can tomato sauce
¼ cup snipped parsley
½ teaspoon dried oregano, crushed
½ teaspoon dried basil, crushed
⅛ teaspoon pepper
1 6½-ounce can minced clams, drained
½ cup dry red wine

● Thaw fish, if frozen. Cut into 1-inch pieces; set aside. In a saucepan combine green pepper, onion, water, and garlic. Cover and cook till vegetables are tender. Stir in *undrained* tomatoes, tomato sauce, parsley, oregano, basil, and pepper.

● Bring to boiling; reduce heat. Cover and simmer for 20 minutes. Add fish. Bring just to boiling; reduce heat. Cover and simmer for 5 to 7 minutes or till fish flakes easily with a fork. Stir in clams and wine, then heat through. Makes 4 servings.

Beef

You've probably heard lots of beefs about beef! But it's the fat winding through the meat (called marbling) that's the biggest concern. If you simply switch to the leanest beef cuts, you'll find plenty to sink your teeth into.

When shopping, read the labels on ground beef before you buy: Look for 85 to 90 percent lean (or 10 to 15 percent fat). Roasts that get a stamp of approval are eye of round, chuck arm, rump, or sirloin tip. Steaks such as eye of round, top round, flank, and sirloin tip make very favorable fat-conscious choices. But beware: All organ meats (liver, kidney, sweetbreads, and brain) are undeniably high in fat and cholesterol.

The way you cook meats also can make or break a low-fat menu. Look for separable fat to slash off before you cook meat. Broil and roast meats on a rack, so unwanted fat drips away while the meat sizzles. Don't forget to be stingy with added fat when browning meat, and diligent in skimming it off from the pan juices.

Sauerbraten with Crab Apples

7 grams fat/serving

Hats off to this German-style pot roast!

1 16-ounce jar spiced crab apples
1 cup red wine vinegar
1 medium onion, sliced
6 whole cloves
1 bay leaf
¼ teaspoon pepper
1 3½- to 4-pound boneless beef rump roast
   Nonstick spray coating
½ cup crushed gingersnaps (8 cookies)
½ cup raisins

● Drain apples, reserving 1 cup syrup. Return apples to jar, then cover and chill. For marinade, combine reserved syrup, vinegar, onion, cloves, bay leaf, and pepper. Bring to boiling; reduce heat. Cover and simmer for 10 minutes; cool. Place roast in a plastic bag, then set the bag in a bowl or baking dish. Pour marinade over the roast. Close bag, then marinate in the refrigerator for 24 hours, turning occasionally. Drain roast, reserving marinade. Pat meat dry with paper towels.

● Spray a Dutch oven with nonstick coating. Brown meat in the Dutch oven. Meanwhile, strain marinade. Discard onion, cloves, and bay leaf. Add 1 cup marinade to meat in Dutch oven. Bring to boiling; reduce heat. Cover and simmer for 2 to 2½ hours or till meat is tender. Transfer to a platter; keep warm.

● Measure pan juices; skim off fat. Add enough water to make 2 cups liquid. Combine liquid, gingersnaps, and raisins. Cook and stir till bubbly. Serve with roast. Garnish with reserved crab apples and watercress, if desired. Makes 12 servings.

Sauerbraten with Crab Apples

Lasagna Sandwiches

7 grams fat/serving

Reheat frozen sandwiches at 400° for 50 to 60 minutes.

¾ pound lean ground beef
¼ cup chopped green pepper
1½ cups tomato sauce
¼ cup *regular* onion soup mix
½ teaspoon dried oregano, crushed
½ teaspoon dried basil, crushed
¾ cup low-fat cottage cheese, drained
¼ cup grated Parmesan cheese
8 individual 6-inch French-style rolls

● In a skillet cook meat and green pepper till meat is brown; drain off fat. Stir in tomato sauce, soup mix, oregano, and basil. Bring to boiling; reduce heat. Cover and simmer for 5 minutes.

● Combine cottage cheese and Parmesan. Cut a thin slice off the top of each roll. Use a fork to hollow out the bottoms of the rolls, leaving ¼-inch shells. (Save excess bread for another use.)

● Spoon *half* of the meat mixture into the roll bottoms. Spoon cheese mixture over meat. Top with remaining meat mixture, then cover with roll tops. Wrap individually in foil. (*Or,* place on a baking sheet. Cover with foil.) Bake in a 400° oven for 20 to 25 minutes or till heated through. Makes 8 servings.

Assembling the sandwiches
After hollowing out the rolls, spoon half of the meat mixture into the bottom of the rolls. Spoon the cheese mixture over the first layer of meat. Then spread remaining meat mixture over the cheese, and cover with the roll tops.

Wrap these sandwiches individually in foil if you won't be eating them all at once. This way you can keep extras warm in the oven or freeze some for later use. But, if you plan to serve all the sandwiches at once, it's easier to heat them covered with foil on a baking sheet.

Vegetable-Stuffed Steaks

4 grams fat/serving

Stuffed shirts, stockings, spuds . . . and now steak!

2 beef top loin steaks,
   cut 1 inch thick
   (about 1 pound total)
   Nonstick spray coating
1 cup sliced fresh mushrooms
2 tablespoons chopped onion
2 tablespoons chopped green
   pepper
2 tablespoons shredded
   carrot
1 small clove garlic, minced
¼ teaspoon Worcestershire
   sauce
   Dash dried thyme, crushed

● Make a pocket in each steak by cutting horizontally into the steak from one side almost to the opposite side. Spray a saucepan with nonstick coating. Add mushrooms, onion, green pepper, carrot, garlic, Worcestershire sauce, and thyme. Cook and stir about 4 minutes or till vegetables are tender.

● Fill each steak pocket with half of the mushroom mixture. Place steaks on a rack in an unheated broiler pan. Broil 4 inches from the heat till desired doneness, turning once. (Allow 16 to 18 minutes total time for medium-rare.) Makes 4 servings.

Southern-Style Round Steak

4 grams fat/serving

Sweet potatoes lend a special Southern charm.

1½ pounds beef round steak,
   cut about ¾ inch thick
   Nonstick spray coating
3 medium sweet potatoes *or*
   yams, peeled and sliced
   ½ inch thick
1 large onion, cut into thin
   wedges
1 medium green pepper, cut
   into ½-inch strips
1 16-ounce can tomatoes,
   cut up
1 teaspoon sugar
½ teaspoon dried thyme,
   crushed
⅛ teaspoon pepper
   Several dashes bottled hot
   pepper sauce
1 tablespoon cornstarch
1 tablespoon cold water

● Cut meat into six serving-size pieces; pound to ¼- to ½-inch thickness. Sprinkle lightly with salt and pepper. Spray a Dutch oven with nonstick coating. Brown meat, half at a time, in the Dutch oven. Return all meat to Dutch oven. Top with sweet potatoes, onion, and green pepper. Stir together *undrained* tomatoes, sugar, thyme, pepper, and hot pepper sauce. Pour over meat and vegetables.

● Cover and bake in a 350° oven for 1¼ to 1½ hours or until meat and vegetables are tender, occasionally spooning sauce over mixture. With a slotted spoon, transfer meat and vegetables to a serving platter; keep warm. Skim fat from pan juices. Stir together cornstarch and water. Add to juices. Cook and stir till thickened and bubbly, then cook and stir 2 minutes more. Spoon over meat and vegetables. Makes 6 servings.

Taco Salad for Two

14 grams fat/serving

A meaty treat for you and your favorite amigo.

2 8-inch flour tortillas
  Nonstick spray coating
6 ounces lean ground beef *or*
   frozen ground raw turkey,
   thawed
½ cup chopped onion
1 clove garlic, minced
1½ teaspoons all-purpose flour
⅔ cup tomato sauce
1 4-ounce can green chili
   peppers, rinsed, seeded,
   and chopped
1 teaspoon chili powder
2 cups torn lettuce
½ cup cherry tomatoes,
   quartered
¼ cup shredded Monterey
   Jack cheese (1 ounce)
   Taco sauce (optional)

● Brush tortillas lightly with water to make them more pliable. Press each tortilla into a small individual casserole sprayed with nonstick coating. Bake in a 350° oven for 15 to 20 minutes or till light brown.

● Meanwhile, cook meat, onion, and garlic till meat is brown and onion is tender; drain well. Stir in flour, then add tomato sauce, green chili peppers, and chili powder. Cook and stir till thickened and bubbly, then cook and stir 1 minute more.

● Arrange lettuce and cherry tomatoes in the tortilla shells. Top with meat mixture, then sprinkle with cheese. Serve with taco sauce, if desired. Makes 2 servings.

Vegetable-Beef Spaghetti Sauce

9 grams fat/serving

Mamma mia! You'll have the best-dressed pasta in town!

¾ pound lean ground beef
2 cups sliced fresh
   mushrooms
1 medium onion, chopped
½ cup chopped green pepper
½ cup thinly sliced carrot
2 cloves garlic, minced
1 28-ounce can tomatoes,
   cut up
1 8-ounce can tomato sauce
½ cup halved and thinly sliced
   zucchini
1 teaspoon dried basil,
   crushed
½ teaspoon sugar
½ teaspoon dried oregano,
   crushed
8 ounces spaghetti *or*
   fettuccine
1 tablespoon cornstarch
1 tablespoon cold water

● In a large saucepan cook ground beef, mushrooms, onion, green pepper, carrot, and garlic till meat is brown and vegetables are tender. Drain off fat. Stir in *undrained* tomatoes, tomato sauce, zucchini, basil, sugar, and oregano. Bring to boiling; reduce heat. Simmer, uncovered, for 10 minutes.

● Meanwhile, cook spaghetti or fettuccine according to package directions; drain. Combine cornstarch and water; add to sauce. Cook and stir till thickened and bubbly, then cook and stir 2 minutes more. Serve sauce over spaghetti. Makes 4 servings.

Taco Salad for Two

Butterflying Meat

A butterfly cut is a boned or boneless cut of meat split almost all the way through the center, then spread open flat. Pound, fill, or roll the meat like the Rolled Roast with Spinach Stuffing on the opposite page. To butterfly a boneless roast, start by slitting the piece of meat lengthwise about halfway through the center. Spread the meat open. At the V formed by the cut, make two more perpendicular lengthwise slits to the right and left of the V. Then, spread the meat open more.

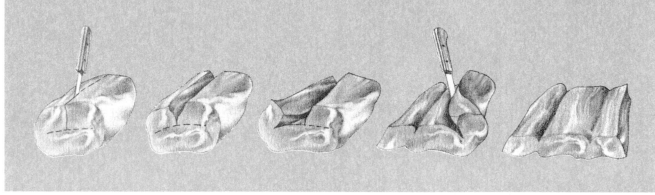

Creamy Pot Roast and Vegetables

6 grams fat/serving

A family feast that features a savory yogurt sauce.

Nonstick spray coating
1 3- to 4-pound beef chuck
   pot roast
¾ cup water
1 teaspoon instant beef
   bouillon granules
1 large bay leaf
4 medium potatoes, peeled
   and quartered, *or* 16
   whole new potatoes
4 medium carrots, cut into
   1-inch lengths
4 stalks celery, bias-sliced
   into ½-inch pieces
2 leeks, sliced, *or*
   1 large onion, sliced
3 tablespoons all-purpose
   flour
½ cup plain low-fat yogurt

● Spray a Dutch oven with nonstick coating. Brown meat in the Dutch oven. Sprinkle with pepper. Combine water and bouillon granules; pour over roast. Add bay leaf. Cover and bake in a 325° oven for 1 hour.

● Add potatoes, carrots, celery, and leeks to Dutch oven. Cover and continue baking for 1½ to 1¾ hours more or till meat and vegetables are tender. Transfer the meat and vegetables to a serving platter; keep warm.

● Discard bay leaf. Skim fat from pan juices, then measure juices. Add enough water to make 1 cup liquid. Stir flour into yogurt. Stir about ¼ *cup* pan juices into yogurt mixture. Add yogurt mixture and remaining pan juices to Dutch oven. Cook and stir till thickened and bubbly, then cook and stir 1 minute more. Spoon some sauce over meat and vegetables. Pass remaining sauce. Makes 8 servings.

Rolled Roast with Spinach Stuffing

For oven roasting, place meat in a 325° oven about 1¼ hours.

1 **2-pound beef eye of round roast, butterflied**
Nonstick spray coating
8 **ounces fresh mushrooms, finely chopped (3 cups)**
¼ **cup finely chopped onion**
1 **clove garlic, minced**
½ **of a 10-ounce package frozen chopped spinach, thawed and well drained**
2 **slightly beaten egg whites**
2 **tablespoons grated Parmesan cheese**
Creamy Yogurt Sauce

● Cover roast with clear plastic wrap; pound with a meat mallet to ½- to ¾-inch thickness. Spray a skillet with nonstick coating. Cook mushrooms, onion, and garlic in the skillet till tender and all mushroom liquid has evaporated. Stir in spinach, egg whites, and cheese; spread over roast. Starting from the short side, roll up jelly-roll style, then tie with string.

● In a covered grill arrange preheated coals around a drip pan; test for *medium-heat* above the pan. Place roast over pan. Lower grill hood. Grill for 1 to 1¼ hours or till meat thermometer registers 140°. Remove from heat, then cover with foil. Let stand 10 minutes; slice meat. Serve with Yogurt Sauce. Serves 8.

Yogurt Sauce: Combine ½ cup plain low-fat *yogurt*, 4 teaspoons all-purpose *flour*, ½ teaspoon instant *beef bouillon granules*, and ⅛ teaspoon *pepper*. Stir in ½ cup *skim milk*. Cook and stir till thickened and bubbly, then cook and stir 1 minute more. Sprinkle with *paprika*.

Rolling the roast
Spread the spinach-mushroom mixture over the roast to within ½ inch of the edges. Leaving a little space around the edges allows you to roll up the roast without the filling oozing out the ends.

To roll the roast, start at the short side of the roast and roll up jelly-roll style. Secure the meat roll with a kitchen string. Tie the roast crosswise at several places to prevent it from coming unrolled during cooking. Remove the string before slicing.

Hearty German Stew
8 grams fat/serving

Granny Smith, Jonathan, or Winesap apples hold up best in this robust, one-dish meal.

Nonstick spray coating
1½ pounds lean beef stew meat,
    cut into 1-inch cubes
1 large cooking apple,
    peeled, cored, and
    chopped
1 medium onion, sliced
1 cup beer
1 cup water
1 tablespoon instant beef
    bouillon granules
2 cloves garlic, minced
2 bay leaves
¾ teaspoon dried thyme,
    crushed
2 large cooking apples,
    cored and *each* cut into
    8 wedges
3 medium carrots, sliced
1 10-ounce package spaetzle
¼ teaspoon poppy seed
¼ cup cold water
1 tablespoon cornstarch

● Spray a large saucepan with nonstick coating. Brown meat in the saucepan. Stir in chopped apple, onion, beer, 1 cup water, bouillon granules, garlic, bay leaves, and thyme. Bring to boiling; reduce heat. Cover and simmer for 1½ hours. Stir in apple wedges and carrots. Cover and simmer for 15 to 20 minutes more or till meat and carrots are tender. Remove bay leaves.

● Meanwhile, cook spaetzle according to package directions; drain. Sprinkle with poppy seed; keep warm. Stir together ¼ cup water and cornstarch, then add to beef mixture. Cook and stir till thickened and bubbly, then cook and stir 2 minutes more. Serve over spaetzle. Makes 6 servings.

Corned Beef Hash
17 grams fat/serving

Try this Test Kitchen tip: Use chilled cooked potatoes to prevent mushiness.

Nonstick spray coating
1 medium onion, finely
    chopped
3 cups finely chopped cooked
    potatoes
¾ pound corned beef,
    ground (2¼ cups)
¼ cup skim milk
1 teaspoon Worcestershire
    sauce
⅛ teaspoon pepper

● Spray a 10-inch ovenproof skillet with nonstick coating. Cook onion in the skillet till tender. Add potatoes, corned beef, milk, Worcestershire sauce, and pepper; mix well. Bake in a 350° oven for 15 to 20 minutes or till hot. Makes 6 servings.

Roast Beef Hash: Prepare Corned Beef Hash as directed above, *except* substitute 2 cups chopped or ground cooked *roast beef* for the corned beef and increase the Worcestershire sauce to *1 tablespoon*. Continue as directed. Bake roast beef mixture about 30 minutes or till hot.

Pork

There's good news for pork lovers. Research shows that much of today's pork is 50 percent leaner than the same product 30 years ago! So you now have more choices than ever before for low-fat eating.

Center-cut ham, loin chops and roasts, pork tenderloin, and Canadian bacon are some of the leanest cuts. A newcomer to the meat counter is ground pork. Unlike ground beef, a package of ground pork may not reveal the fat content. But chances are the pork came from the shoulder, which is 70 to 80 percent lean. Your butcher should know more about the specific fat content.

Be sparing with pork cuts and products that are naturally high in fat. You know them—bacon, sausage, and spareribs. Most of their flavor comes from fat, which is a whopping 75 percent or more of the product.

Pork Harvest Dinner

15 grams fat/serving

The "harvest" ingredients: apples and winter squash.

Nonstick spray coating
1 2-pound pork sirloin roast
1 6-ounce can frozen apple juice concentrate, thawed
½ cup chopped onion
½ cup chopped celery
1 teaspoon instant chicken bouillon granules
6 whole allspice
4 whole black peppercorns
1 bay leaf
1 pound piece of butternut *or* other winter squash
2 large apples
Lemon juice
1 tablespoon cold water
1 tablespoon vinegar
2 teaspoons cornstarch

● Spray a Dutch oven with nonstick coating. Brown meat in the Dutch oven. Add apple juice concentrate, onion, celery, bouillon granules, allspice, peppercorns, and bay leaf. Bring to boiling, then reduce heat. Cover and simmer about 1 hour or until meat is almost tender.

● Meanwhile, remove seeds and membranes from squash. Cut into ½-inch slices. Remove peel, then halve or quarter the slices. Core apples and cut into eighths, then brush with lemon juice.

● Add squash to the Dutch oven. Cover; simmer for 10 minutes. Add apples, then cover and simmer about 10 minutes more or until meat and squash are tender. Transfer meat, squash, and apples to a platter. Keep warm. Strain pan juices and discard allspice, peppercorns, and bay leaf. Skim fat from juices. Measure juices and add enough water to make 1 cup liquid. Return to Dutch oven.

● Stir together water, vinegar, and cornstarch; add to pan juices. Cook and stir till thickened and bubbly, then cook and stir 2 minutes more. Serve with meat. Makes 4 servings.

Pork with Papaya

Pork with Papaya

Pop the peppery papaya seeds in a blender and coarsely grind them to sprinkle on salads or to use as a fat-free garnish.

1 pound lean boneless pork
  Nonstick spray coating
3 cloves garlic, minced
2 cups broccoli flowerets
4 green onions, bias-sliced
  into 1-inch pieces
½ cup water
¼ cup soy sauce
1 medium papaya
2 tablespoons cornstarch
2 tablespoons cold water
2 medium tomatoes, chopped
3 cups hot cooked brown rice
¼ cup sliced green onion

● Partially freeze meat. Cut on the bias into thin bite-size strips. Spray a 12-inch skillet with nonstick coating. Cook pork and garlic in the skillet till meat is brown, stirring occasionally. Stir in broccoli, bias-sliced onions, ½ cup water, and soy sauce. Bring to boiling, then reduce heat. Cover and simmer for 3 to 5 minutes or until broccoli is crisp-tender and meat is done.

● Meanwhile, quarter papaya lengthwise, then seed and peel. Cut crosswise into ¼-inch slices. Stir together cornstarch and 2 tablespoons water, then add to skillet. Cook and stir till thickened and bubbly, then cook and stir 2 minutes more. Stir in papaya and tomatoes and heat through. Toss together rice and sliced onion. Serve with pork mixture. Makes 6 servings.

Pork Pastitsio

A Greek extravaganza layered with pasta, spiced meat, and cheese-flavored custard.

6 ounces elbow macaroni
  (1½ cups)
2 slightly beaten egg whites
⅓ cup grated Parmesan cheese
¼ cup skim milk
1 pound lean ground pork
½ cup chopped onion
1 8-ounce can tomato sauce
½ teaspon ground cinnamon
⅛ teaspoon ground nutmeg
⅛ teaspoon pepper
1 cup skim milk
1 tablespoon cornstarch
1 beaten egg
¼ cup grated Parmesan cheese

● Cook macaroni according to package directions. Drain. Stir together macaroni, egg whites, ⅓ cup Parmesan, and ¼ cup milk. Set aside. In a skillet cook pork and onion until meat is brown and onion is tender. Drain off fat. Stir in tomato sauce, cinnamon, nutmeg, and pepper.

● For sauce, in a medium saucepan combine 1 cup milk and cornstarch. Cook and stir till thickened and bubbly. Remove from heat. Stir about *half* of the hot mixture into the beaten egg, then return all to saucepan. Stir in ¼ cup Parmesan.

● Place *half* of the macaroni mixture in an 8x8x2-inch baking dish. Spoon meat mixture over, then add remaining macaroni mixture. Cover with sauce. Bake in a 350° oven for 40 to 45 minutes or till bubbly. Let stand 10 minutes before serving. Makes 6 servings.

Pork Bundle Kabobs

7 grams fat/serving

Instead of grilling, place skewers on a rack in an unheated broiler pan. Broil 4 inches from the heat for 7 to 8 minutes or until done, turning once.

¾ pound lean boneless pork,
　　cut 1 inch thick
¼ cup orange juice
¼ cup soy sauce
1 tablespoon brown sugar
1 teaspoon grated gingerroot
1 10-ounce package frozen
　　asparagus spears
2 medium carrots, cut into
　　3-inch sticks

● Partially freeze meat. Cut on the bias into 3-inch strips. For marinade, combine orange juice, soy sauce, sugar, and gingerroot. Place meat in a plastic bag, then set in a bowl. Pour marinade over meat and close bag. Marinate in the refrigerator for 4 to 6 hours or overnight, turning bag occasionally.

● Cook each vegetable *separately* in a small amount of water about 5 minutes or till crisp-tender. Drain and cool slightly. Cut asparagus in half crosswise. Drain meat, reserving marinade.

● For each bundle, wrap a meat strip around one or two asparagus pieces and one carrot stick. Repeat with remaining meat and vegetables. Thread bundles, ladder fashion, on two parallel skewers. Brush with reserved marinade.

● Grill over *medium* coals for 4 minutes. Turn and grill for 3 to 4 minutes more or till done, brushing with marinade. Serves 4.

Assembling the kabobs

To assemble the kabobs, wrap the meat strips around the pieces of asparagus and carrot. Secure bundles with toothpicks, if necessary.

Thread the pork bundles, ladder fashion, on two separate parallel skewers. Or, use skewers that are connected to form double skewers. You'll need two skewers to hold the oblong meat and vegetable bundles together during grilling.

Corn-Stuffed Pork Chops

15 grams fat/serving

Piled full with a south-of-the-border calico stuffing.

6 pork loin chops, cut 1¼ inches thick
¼ cup chopped green pepper
1 small onion, chopped
1 tablespoon water
2 slightly beaten egg whites
1 slice whole wheat *or* rye bread, toasted and cubed (¾ cup)
½ cup canned whole kernel corn
2 tablespoons chopped pimiento
¼ teaspoon ground cumin
⅛ teaspoon salt
⅛ teaspoon pepper
¼ cup apple juice *or* cider

● Make a pocket in each chop by cutting horizontally into the chop from one side almost to the opposite side. For stuffing, in a saucepan combine green pepper, onion, and water. Cover and cook till tender. Combine egg whites, bread, corn, pimiento, cumin, salt, and pepper, then toss with onion mixture.

● Spoon about *¼ cup* stuffing into *each* chop. Securely fasten opening with toothpicks. Place on a rack in a roasting pan. Bake in a 350° oven for 45 to 50 minutes or till tender, brushing occasionally with apple juice. Before serving, remove toothpicks. Makes 6 servings.

Pork Chop-Vegetable Skillet

12 grams fat/serving

Nonstick spray coating
4 pork loin chops, cut ½ inch thick
2 medium potatoes, peeled, halved lengthwise, and sliced
1 16-ounce can stewed tomatoes
¼ cup chopped onion
¼ cup finely chopped celery
1 tablespoon snipped parsley
1 teaspoon instant beef bouillon granules
¾ teaspoon dried sage, crushed
1 medium zucchini, sliced
1 tablespoon cold water
2 teaspoons cornstarch

● Spray a large skillet with nonstick coating. Brown chops on both sides in the skillet for 15 minutes. Remove chops, then drain off fat. Place potatoes in skillet and top with meat. Combine tomatoes, onion, celery, parsley, bouillon granules, and sage, then pour over meat and potatoes. Cover and cook over medium-low heat for 20 minutes. Add zucchini, and cover and cook about 10 minutes more or until meat and vegetables are tender. Remove meat and vegetables and keep warm.

● Skim any excess fat from pan juices; measure juices. Add enough water to make ¾ cup liquid; return to skillet. Stir together water and cornstarch and add to skillet. Cook and stir till thickened and bubbly, then cook and stir 2 minutes more. Spoon over meat and vegetables. Makes 4 servings.

Garden Ham Brunch Crepes

5 grams fat/serving

Rise and shine! These wine-sauced eye-openers are worth it.

12 Low-Fat Crepes (see recipe, below)
 1 cup frozen chopped broccoli
    Nonstick spray coating
 1 tablespoon chopped onion
 1 cup skim milk
 1 tablespoon cornstarch
 ¼ teaspoon finely shredded lemon peel
 ⅛ teaspoon paprika
 ¼ cup shredded American cheese (1 ounce)
 1 tablespoon dry white wine
1½ cups diced fully cooked lean ham
 ¾ cup shredded lettuce
 ¼ cup snipped parsley

● Prepare Low-Fat Crepes. Cook broccoli according to package directions; drain. For sauce, spray a saucepan with nonstick coating. Cook onion in the saucepan until tender. Combine milk and cornstarch and add to saucepan. Add lemon peel and paprika. Cook and stir till thickened and bubbly, then cook and stir 2 minutes more. Add cheese and wine. Stir till cheese melts.

● For filling, combine ham, lettuce, parsley, broccoli, and ½ *cup* sauce. Cover remaining sauce and set aside. To assemble, spoon about ¼ *cup* filling along the center of unbrowned side of *each* crepe. Fold two opposite edges to overlap filling. Fold remaining edges together to form a square packet.

● Spray a 12x7½x2-inch baking dish with nonstick coating. Place crepes, seam side down, in dish. Cover with foil and bake in a 375° oven about 20 minutes or till heated through. Reheat remaining sauce and spoon over crepes. Makes 6 servings.

Low-Fat Crepes

1 gram fat/serving

Light as a feather!

 ½ cup all-purpose flour
 ½ cup whole wheat flour
1½ cups skim milk
 1 egg
 1 egg white
    Nonstick spray coating

● Combine all-purpose flour and whole wheat flour, then add milk, egg, and egg white. Beat with a rotary beater till blended.

● Spray a 6-inch skillet with nonstick coating, then heat the skillet. Remove from heat and spoon in about *2 tablespoons* batter. Lift and tilt skillet to spread batter. Return to heat and brown on one side only. Invert pan over paper towels to remove crepe. Repeat to make about 18 crepes, lightly greasing skillet occasionally. (*Don't* spray *hot* skillet with nonstick coating.) Makes about 18 crepes.

Note: To freeze, stack crepes with two layers of waxed paper between crepes. Overwrap the stack in a moisture-and vaporproof bag, then place in a plastic container. Freeze up to four months. Thaw crepes at room temperature about 1 hour before using.

Orange Sticky Rolls
(see recipe, page 56)

Garden Ham Brunch Crepes

Lamb

Several parts of lamb are a cut above the rest when it comes to fat-watching. The leanest portion of lamb is the leg. Be sure to trim away the heavy covering of fat on the outside of the leg before cooking, though.

Cuts from the leg include the lamb leg sirloin chop, center roast, center slice, and shank. The shank is fattier than the other cuts from the leg, but you can easily trim off most of the fat before cooking. If leg chops aren't available, choose loin or rib chops instead.

Herbed Lamb Roast

7 grams fat/serving

1 2½- to 3-pound boneless center-cut leg of lamb
1 small onion, finely chopped
¼ cup finely chopped celery
¼ cup shredded carrot
2 tablespoons Dijon-style mustard
1 tablespoon plain low-fat yogurt
¼ teaspoon dried thyme, crushed
¼ teaspoon dried rosemary, crushed
1 tablespoon cornstarch
½ teaspoon instant chicken bouillon granules

● Unroll roast and sprinkle lightly with pepper. Combine onion, celery, carrot, mustard, yogurt, thyme, and rosemary, then spread over roast. Roll up and tie securely. Place roast on a rack in a shallow roasting pan. Insert meat thermometer in the thickest portion of the meat.

● Roast in a 325° oven for 1½ to 1¾ hours or till thermometer registers 150°. Let stand 15 minutes. Remove string and slice. Skim fat from pan juices, then measure juices. Add enough water to make ¼ cup liquid, then place in a saucepan. Stir together ¾ cup *cold water*, cornstarch, and bouillon granules. Add to pan juices. Cook and stir till thickened and bubbly; cook and stir 2 minutes more. Serve with meat. Makes 6 servings.

Orange-Sauced Lamb Chops

4 grams fat/serving

4 lamb leg sirloin chops, cut ¾ inch thick (about 1 pound total)
1 teaspoon finely shredded orange peel
½ cup orange juice
½ teaspoon instant chicken bouillon granules
¼ teaspoon ground nutmeg
   Nonstick spray coating
3 inches stick cinnamon
2 tablespoons cold water
2 teaspoons cornstarch
2 orange slices, halved

● Arrange chops in a shallow dish. For marinade, combine peel, juice, bouillon granules, and nutmeg. Cook and stir till granules dissolve; pour over chops. Cover and marinate in the refrigerator for several hours or overnight, turning chops occasionally.

● Drain chops, reserving marinade. Spray a skillet with non-stick coating. Brown chops on both sides in the skillet. Add reserved marinade and cinnamon. Bring to boiling, then reduce heat. Cover and simmer about 30 minutes or till meat is tender. Remove meat and keep warm. Discard cinnamon.

● Stir together water and cornstarch. Add to skillet. Cook and stir till thickened and bubbly; cook and stir 2 minutes more. Add orange slices; heat through. Spoon over chops. Serves 4.

Sweet and Sour Lamb

1 pound lean boneless lamb
1 8-ounce can pineapple
    chunks (juice pack)
3 tablespoons vinegar
2 tablespoons tomato sauce
4 teaspoons cornstarch
1 tablespoon brown sugar
1 teaspoon instant chicken
    bouillon granules
    Nonstick spray coating
1 medium green pepper,
    cut into strips
4 green onions, bias-sliced
    into 1-inch pieces
½ cup shredded carrot
2 cloves garlic, minced
½ cup sliced water chestnuts
2 cups hot cooked rice

● Partially freeze lamb. Cut on the bias into thin bite-size strips; set aside. Drain pineapple, reserving juice. Add enough water to to juice to make ¾ cup liquid. Stir in vinegar, tomato sauce, cornstarch, sugar, and bouillon granules.

● Spray a wok or large skillet with nonstick coating. Cook green pepper, onions, carrot, and garlic in the wok about 3 minutes or till crisp-tender. Remove from wok. Cook lamb, half at a time, in wok about 3 minutes or till tender. (Add 1 teaspoon *cooking oil*, if necessary, to prevent sticking.) Drain off any fat.

● Return all meat and vegetables to wok. Stir cornstarch mixture, then add to wok. Cook and stir till thickened and bubbly, then cook and stir 2 minutes more. Stir in water chestnuts and pineapple; heat through. Serve over rice. Makes 4 servings.

Dividing a Leg of Lamb

A leg of lamb is the leanest portion of the lamb, making it a great choice to use in a variety of recipes. Have your butcher cut a 7- to 10-pound whole leg of lamb roughly into thirds.

The shank end is a good piece to cut into cubes or strips. Use this when a recipe calls for lean boneless lamb, such as the Sweet and Sour Lamb, above.

The middle portion of the leg, or center-cut lamb roast, is a good size for small families. See the recipe for Herbed Lamb Roast on the opposite page.

Have the butcher cut the large end of the leg of lamb into four chops. Put them to good use in the Orange-Sauced Lamb Chops on the opposite page.

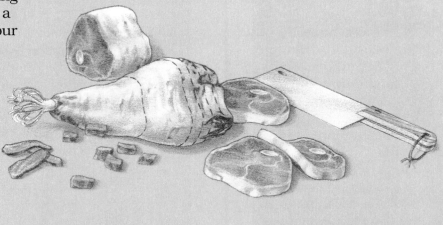

Veal

Fat that weaves its way throughout portions of beef (called marbling) can create problems in a low-fat menu. But veal is a different story. Because it's the young and tender meat of a calf that has not yet put on adult fat, veal cuts are surprisingly lean. The only exception is the breast, where most of the fat is located.

Fruited Veal Marsala

6 grams fat/serving

Marsala, the most famous wine of Sicily, is a sweet yet robust fortified wine.

2 cups fresh *or* one 10-ounce package frozen brussels sprouts
3 stalks celery, bias-sliced into 1-inch pieces
1 pound boneless veal leg round steak, cut ¼ inch thick
Nonstick spray coating
⅓ cup orange juice
⅓ cup dry Marsala *or* sherry
½ teaspoon instant chicken bouillon granules
1 small bay leaf
1 cup seedless grapes, halved

● Cook brussels sprouts and celery in a small amount of boiling water about 10 minutes or till crisp-tender. Drain and keep warm. Halve any large sprouts.

● Cut veal into six serving-size pieces, then pound to ⅛-inch thickness. Spray a large skillet with nonstick coating. Cook meat in the skillet about 1 minute on each side or until tender. Transfer meat to a platter and keep warm.

● Add orange juice, Marsala, bouillon granules, bay leaf, and 2 tablespoons *water* to skillet. Bring to boiling; reduce heat. Simmer, uncovered, about 5 minutes or till reduced to about ¼ cup. Add grapes, then simmer about 1 minute more or till hot. Discard bay leaf. Spoon over meat and vegetables. Serves 6.

Veal-Barley Stew

7 grams fat/serving

1 pound lean boneless veal
Nonstick spray coating
3 cups sliced fresh mushrooms
12 small whole onions
1 clove garlic, minced
2 12-ounce cans vegetable juice cocktail
4 medium carrots, sliced
2 stalks celery, sliced
1 medium parsnip, sliced
1 medium potato, cubed
¼ cup pearl barley
1 bay leaf
½ teaspoon dried basil, crushed

● Cut veal into ¾-inch cubes. Spray a Dutch oven with nonstick coating. Brown veal in the Dutch oven; remove. Cook mushrooms, onions, and garlic in Dutch oven about 5 minutes or until mushrooms are tender. Drain off any fat.

● Stir in meat, vegetable juice cocktail, carrots, celery, parsnip, potato, barley, bay leaf, and basil. Bring to boiling, then reduce heat. Cover and simmer about 45 minutes or until vegetables and barley are tender. Discard bay leaf. Makes 6 servings.

Fruited Veal Marsala

Meatless Eating

Going meatless doesn't necessarily mean you'll be going fatless! It's a challenge when you consider that the usual meatless alternatives—eggs and cheese—are high in both fat and cholesterol. We've found some easy-to-swallow answers, however. A generous mix of low-fat proteins such as tofu; fat-skimmed dairy products; more egg whites and fewer egg yolks; and beans, peas, and lentils fulfills a meatless menu nicely.

Fat and optimum protein requirements were figured into every recipe in this main-dish section. So rest assured that the recipes here will be ideally suited to your fat-conscious and meatless eating style.

Spicy Bean Tostadas

7 grams fat/serving

Corn tortillas get our vote because they have less fat than flour tortillas.

- 1 15½-ounce can red kidney beans, drained and rinsed
- 1 14½-ounce can yellow hominy, drained
- 1 10-ounce can tomatoes and green chili peppers
- 1 8-ounce can tomato sauce
- ½ cup sliced celery
- ½ cup chopped onion
- 1 tablespoon snipped parsley
- ½ teaspoon sugar
- 1 tablespoon cold water
- 1 teaspoon cornstarch
- 4 8-inch corn tortillas
- 2 cups shredded lettuce
- 2 medium tomatoes, chopped
- ½ cup shredded cheddar cheese (2 ounces)
- ½ cup plain low-fat yogurt

● In a large saucepan combine kidney beans, hominy, tomatoes and green chili peppers, tomato sauce, celery, onion, parsley, and sugar. Bring to boiling; reduce heat. Cover and simmer for 10 minutes. Stir together cold water and cornstarch; add to the saucepan. Cook and stir till thickened and bubbly, then cook and stir 2 minutes more.

● Meanwhile, place tortillas in a single layer on a baking sheet. Bake in a 350° oven for 10 to 15 minutes or till crisp. Place each tortilla on a serving plate. Spoon bean mixture on tortillas, then sprinkle with lettuce, tomatoes, and cheese. Dollop with yogurt. Serve with taco sauce, if desired. Makes 4 servings.

Open-Face Vegewiches

The best use of tofu this side of the Orient!

Nonstick spray coating
1 16-ounce package tofu
   (fresh bean curd), drained
4 1-ounce slices cheddar
   cheese, halved
1 medium onion, thinly sliced
   and separated into rings
1 cup sliced fresh mushrooms
½ cup thinly sliced carrot
½ cup thinly sliced celery
2 tablespoons water
1 tablespoon Worcestershire
   sauce
½ teaspoon cornstarch
8 ½-inch slices French bread,
   toasted

● Spray the rack of an unheated broiler pan with nonstick coating. Cut tofu into eight ½-inch slices, then place on the rack. Broil about 4 inches from the heat for 4 minutes. Turn and broil 1 to 2 minutes more or till light brown. Top each tofu slice with half of a cheese slice. Broil about 1 minute more or till cheese melts.

● Meanwhile, spray a saucepan with nonstick coating. Cook onion, mushrooms, carrot, and celery in the saucepan till tender. Combine water, Worcestershire sauce, and cornstarch; stir into vegetables. Cook and stir till thickened and bubbly, then cook and stir 1 minute more.

● To assemble sandwiches, place tofu on bread slices. Transfer to individual serving plates, then spoon vegetable mixture over sandwiches. Makes 4 servings.

Cheese and Spinach Casseroles

A cousin of quiche, with a cautious eye on cholesterol.

2 cups low-fat cottage cheese
3 egg whites
⅓ cup all-purpose flour
¾ teaspoon dried basil,
   crushed
⅛ teaspoon garlic powder
⅛ teaspoon pepper
8 ounces fresh spinach, torn
   (6 cups)
1 cup shredded mozzarella
   cheese (4 ounces)
1 8-ounce can water
   chestnuts, drained
   and chopped
   Nonstick spray coating
1 medium tomato, cut into
   8 thin slices

● In a blender container or food processor bowl combine cottage cheese and egg whites. Cover and blend till smooth. Stir together flour, basil, garlic powder, and pepper. Add cottage cheese mixture and mix well. Stir in spinach, *half* of the mozzarella cheese, and water chestnuts.

● Spray four au gratin dishes with nonstick coating. Spoon spinach mixture into the dishes, then place on a baking sheet. Cover loosely with foil. Bake in a 350° oven about 30 minutes or until a knife inserted near the center comes out clean. Arrange two tomato slices over each dish, then sprinkle with remaining mozzarella cheese. Bake about 3 minutes more or till cheese melts. Makes 4 servings.

Tamale Lentil Soup

6 grams fat/serving

A meatless meal with stick-to-your-ribs goodness. (Pictured on the front cover.)

½ cup dry lentils
3½ cups water
1 cup frozen whole kernel corn
1 cup frozen cut green beans
1 cup sliced zucchini *or* yellow summer squash
1 cup sliced celery
1 cup sliced carrot
1 8-ounce can stewed tomatoes
1 7¾-ounce can semi-condensed tomato soup
½ cup chopped onion
½ cup chopped green pepper
1 clove garlic, minced
¾ teaspoon chili powder
¼ teaspoon ground cumin
⅛ teaspoon pepper
Tamale Topper
½ cup shredded cheddar cheese (2 ounces)

● In a Dutch oven combine uncooked lentils and *1½ cups* water. Bring to boiling; reduce the heat. Cover and simmer for 20 minutes, then drain. Stir in remaining water, corn, beans, zucchini, celery, carrot, tomatoes, tomato soup, onion, green pepper, garlic, chili powder, cumin, and pepper. Return to boiling, then reduce heat. Cover and simmer about 20 minutes or until vegetables are almost tender.

● Drop Tamale Topper in six mounds onto the hot stew. Cover and simmer about 20 minutes or till topper is done. Sprinkle with cheese. Makes 6 servings.

Tamale Topper: In a saucepan place ¾ cup *cornmeal.* Gradually stir in 1¼ cups *skim milk.* Cook and stir till thickened and bubbly. Remove from heat, then stir in a beaten *egg.*

Defatting Broths, Stews, and Gravies

Here's the slickest trick ever for removing fat from cooking liquid. Plan to prepare the food several hours or a day ahead and chill it. Then, before reheating the food, simply lift off the hardened fat that has formed on the surface. When there's no time to chill the liquid, float a few ice cubes on the surface of the warm liquid to harden the fat. Then remove the hardened fat with a spoon.

Another way to remove fat from small amounts of liquid (2 cups or less) is to use a specially designed measuring cup that has the spout at the bottom. Since fat rises to the top, you can pour off the fat-free liquid and leave the fat layer in the measuring cup.

Tamale Lentil Soup

Tamale Lentil Soup

	FAT (g)	CHOLESTEROL (mg)	UNSATURATED FAT (g)	CALORIES	PROTEIN (g)	CARBOHYDRATES (g)	SODIUM (mg)	POTASSIUM (mg)	PROTEIN	VITAMIN A	VITAMIN C	THIAMINE	RIBOFLAVIN	NIACIN	CALCIUM	IRON
				Per Serving					Percent USRDA Per Serving							
MAIN DISHES · POULTRY																
Almond Chicken à l'Orange (p. 15)	11	90	8	499	46	53	833	900	70	41	69	34	22	83	10	31
Barbecued Oven-Fried Chicken (p. 12)	4	73	3	179	22	13	284	345	34	2	1	6	12	38	2	12
Broiled Turkey with Raspberry Sauce (p. 17)	4	70	2	218	30	14	222	448	47	2	24	4	10	52	2	8
Chicken Chowder in Bread Bowls (p. 13)	3	71	2	267	36	22	417	908	55	50	21	9	24	53	30	11
Chicken Couscous (p. 10)	5	73	2	365	27	54	350	1010	42	81	84	21	17	52	8	26
Chicken Enchiladas (p. 14)	10	53	2	354	23	43	592	279	35	20	23	6	19	34	17	19
Chicken Tetrazzini (p. 14)	6	81	3	342	38	30	313	672	59	3	29	15	25	65	16	14
Chicken-Vegetable Stew (p. 9)	12	89	9	390	30	40	530	765	46	43	61	19	23	52	14	19
Curried Turkey Salad (p. 17)	7	67	5	196	23	9	193	408	36	7	32	5	11	28	4	10
Curry Country Chicken (p. 10)	4	73	2	273	24	35	162	575	36	21	58	14	13	48	4	16
Individual Bread Bowls (p. 12)	4	1	2	239	8	44	73	180	13	2	1	20	20	13	7	9
FISH AND SEAFOOD																
Baked Stuffed Whitefish (p. 19)	10	59	4	233	23	12	201	464	35	83	25	14	10	20	6	7
Cioppino-Style Stew (p. 23)	1	70	0	175	22	15	878	706	34	40	91	10	12	24	7	22
Citrus Salmon Steaks (p. 22)	12	80	9	220	26	3	138	631	41	14	29	85	6	53	2	5
Halibut Steaks with Sherry Sauce (p. 19)	11	65	8	188	22	2	123	479	33	12	3	6	7	43	3	5
Sole En Papillote (p. 20)	4	61	2	130	18	3	106	600	28	4	10	7	13	17	8	7
Spicy Asparagus Fish Rolls (p. 18)	8	75	4	201	24	9	270	840	36	33	69	17	18	19	20	13
Tuna-Mac Casserole (p. 22)	3	41	2	254	23	32	500	428	36	33	13	25	16	50	10	14
BEEF																
Beef Stroganoff (low-fat, p. 87)	8	64	4	336	28	35	242	561	43	6	9	28	31	37	10	22
Beef Stroganoff (standard, p. 87)	59	166	24	766	25	33	342	506	38	23	9	27	29	35	10	21
Corned Beef Hash (p. 32)	17	54	8	271	15	13	554	292	23	1	23	6	9	9	3	12
Creamy Pot Roast and Vegetables (p. 30)	6	80	3	258	29	20	158	721	45	81	32	12	17	27	6	23
Hearty German Stew (p. 32)	8	70	3	425	30	54	303	522	46	81	12	34	24	35	5	27
Lasagna Sandwiches (p. 26)	7	41	4	321	20	43	1000	208	30	9	15	22	19	23	9	16
Roast Beef Hash (p. 32)	3	43	2	151	16	13	67	372	25	0	23	7	9	16	3	12
Rolled Roast with Spinach Stuffing (p. 31)	5	55	2	151	21	5	109	362	33	22	7	6	22	20	8	15
Sauerbraten with Crab Apples (p. 24)	7	68	3	194	22	10	81	339	33	0	1	5	10	20	2	18

	FAT (g)	CHOLESTEROL (mg)	UNSATURATED FAT (g)	CALORIES	PROTEIN (g)	CARBOHYDRATES (g)	SODIUM (mg)	POTASSIUM (mg)	PROTEIN	VITAMIN A	VITAMIN C	THIAMINE	RIBOFLAVIN	NIACIN	CALCIUM	IRON
				Per Serving					Percent USRDA Per Serving							
BEEF (continued)																
Southern-Style Round Steak (p. 27)	4	59	2	246	23	28	160	646	35	148	79	12	14	25	5	20
Taco Salad for Two (p. 28)	14	75	5	376	27	36	694	945	42	61	117	16	25	35	21	33
Vegetable-Beef Spaghetti Sauce (p. 28)	9	60	3	460	29	66	726	1120	45	129	117	52	38	56	6	33
Vegetable-Stuffed Steaks (p. 27)	4	38	2	103	13	2	40	247	20	8	13	4	11	16	1	10
PORK																
Corn-Stuffed Pork Chops (p. 37)	15	87	8	301	32	7	159	432	50	4	23	76	22	35	2	24
Garden Ham Brunch Crepes (p. 38)	5	36	2	131	14	7	108	345	22	26	51	19	15	12	11	11
Lasagna (low-fat, p. 86)	12	102	5	342	30	27	615	497	46	31	32	22	26	23	31	17
Lasagna (standard, p. 86)	33	164	13	517	28	27	719	471	43	42	30	31	30	17	47	14
Low-Fat Crepes (p. 38)	1	14	0	38	2	6	17	42	3	1	0	4	5	2	3	1
Pork Bundle Kabobs (p. 36)	7	40	3	170	16	11	1368	535	25	92	47	28	17	18	5	21
Pork Chop-Vegetable Skillet (p. 37)	12	76	6	308	28	20	336	917	44	24	71	71	22	39	4	25
Pork Harvest Dinner (p. 33)	15	87	7	474	33	55	214	1395	50	106	186	88	30	40	8	29
Pork Pastitsio (p. 35)	10	88	4	302	23	30	417	316	35	11	7	36	26	22	19	15
Pork with Papaya (p. 35)	7	36	3	271	16	37	1188	540	24	37	108	27	15	21	7	17
LAMB																
Herbed Lamb Roast (p. 40)	7	88	3	181	26	3	183	341	40	10	3	10	16	28	3	12
Orange-Sauced Lamb Chops (p. 40)	4	49	1	216	17	27	95	303	27	2	38	13	11	22	2	12
Sweet and Sour Lamb (p. 41)	6	59	2	301	19	42	225	421	29	52	78	20	13	24	4	15
VEAL																
Fruited Veal Marsala (p. 42)	6	54	3	177	17	12	109	513	27	8	102	8	14	18	4	15
Veal-Barley Stew (p. 42)	7	50	3	236	18	26	303	924	28	71	44	15	24	33	6	19
MEATLESS																
Cheese and Spinach Casseroles (p. 45)	8	25	2	276	30	23	710	684	47	143	83	13	35	8	37	19
Open-Face Vegewiches (p. 45)	15	28	7	317	20	27	471	378	31	88	12	16	20	11	40	20
Spicy Bean Tostadas (p. 44)	7	16	2	367	17	63	860	790	26	45	56	19	18	16	28	28
Tamale Lentil Soup (p. 46)	6	53	3	268	14	43	529	732	21	85	68	18	19	12	20	17

Side dishes may play second
fiddle in many meals, but
they're real lifesavers in a low-fat
menu. Fat-shy vegetables,
fruits, and grains make
satisfying supporting acts. So
what if pasta, potatoes,
and broccoli with cheese sauce
are your favorites? Our
fat-skimming techniques
prove them entirely possible!
So are our vegetable casseroles,
creamy salad dressings, and
quick breads.

Rice and Pasta

Rice Medley with Vegetables

1 gram fat/serving

Wild rice isn't rice at all. It's the seed of marsh grass that is cultivated or found growing wild along lakes, in streams, and in swampy areas.

¼ cup wild rice
1 cup water
½ cup chopped onion
¼ cup brown rice
1 4-ounce can sliced
    mushrooms
2 small cloves garlic, minced
1 teaspoon instant beef
    bouillon granules
1 medium sweet yellow *or*
    green pepper, coarsely
    chopped

● Run cold water over *uncooked* wild rice in a strainer for 1 minute, lifting rice with fingers to rinse well. In a medium saucepan combine wild rice, water, onion, brown rice, mushrooms, garlic, and bouillon granules.

● Bring to boiling; reduce heat. Cover and simmer for 40 minutes. Stir in chopped pepper. Cover and simmer about 10 minutes more or until rice is tender. Makes 4 servings.

Bulgur-Rice Pilaf

0 grams fat/serving

The precooked cracked wheat (bulgur) adds a nutty flavor to this easy rice dish.

1⅓ cups water
½ cup bulgur wheat
½ cup chopped carrot
½ cup chopped celery
½ cup chopped onion
¼ cup long grain rice
1 teaspoon instant beef
    bouillon granules
¼ teaspoon salt
¼ teaspoon celery seed
⅛ teaspoon pepper

● In a 1½- or 2-quart saucepan combine water, bulgur, carrot, celery, onion, rice, bouillon granules, salt, celery seed, and pepper. Bring to boiling, then reduce heat. Cover and simmer about 20 minutes or till bulgur and rice are tender. Makes 8 servings.

Vegetable-Bordered Pasta Bake

7 grams fat/serving

Broccoli flowerets make an impressive border for this picnic or party take-along.

- 4 ounces whole wheat spaghetti *or* fettuccine
- 1 10-ounce package frozen chopped broccoli
- ½ cup chopped onion
- ¼ cup chopped green *or* sweet red pepper
- 1 clove garlic, minced
- 1 tablespoon margarine
- 1 tablespoon cornstarch
- 1 cup skim milk
- ¾ cup shredded American cheese (3 ounces)
- 1 8-ounce can water chestnuts, drained and coarsely chopped
- 2 cups cooked vegetables

● Break pasta into 1-inch pieces. Cook pasta according to package directions, then drain. In a covered saucepan, cook broccoli, onion, green or sweet red pepper, and garlic in a small amount of water about 10 minutes or till broccoli is crisp-tender; drain.

● Meanwhile, for sauce, in a small saucepan melt margarine. Stir in cornstarch, ¼ teaspoon *salt*, and ⅛ teaspoon *pepper*. Add milk. Cook and stir till thickened and bubbly, then cook and stir 2 minutes more. Add cheese, stirring to melt.

● Stir together sauce, broccoli mixture, pasta, and water chestnuts. Transfer to a 10x6x2-inch baking dish. Arrange cooked vegetables around the dish. Cover and bake in a 350° oven about 30 minutes or until heated through. Makes 6 servings.

Assembling the casserole
Transfer the pasta mixture to the baking dish, then arrange the desired cooked vegetables around the outside edge of the mixture.

Vegetable borders are an easy, fat-free way to dress up almost any casserole, unlike buttered crumbs or other toppings, which contain fat.

Spinach-Herb Fettuccine

2 grams fat/serving

4 ounces spinach fettuccine
   or linguini
2 tablespoons finely chopped
   onion
1 teaspoon margarine
1½ teaspoons cornstarch
1 teaspoon dried basil,
   crushed
½ teaspoon instant chicken
   bouillon granules
⅛ teaspoon garlic powder
   Dash pepper
⅓ cup skim milk
⅓ cup water
2 tablespoons grated
   Parmesan cheese

● Cook pasta according to package directions, then drain. Keep warm. Meanwhile, in a small saucepan cook onion in margarine till tender. Stir in cornstarch, basil, bouillon granules, garlic powder, and pepper. Add milk and water. Cook and stir till thickened and bubbly, then cook and stir 2 minutes more. Toss with pasta. Sprinkle with cheese. Makes 4 servings.

Baked Spinach Gnocchi

3 grams fat/serving

Gnocchi (NAH kee) is an Italian-style dumpling or appetizer made with farina, semolina, puff pastry dough, or potatoes.

1 10-ounce package frozen
   chopped spinach
2 cups skim milk
½ cup quick-cooking farina
2 slightly beaten egg whites
½ cup grated Parmesan cheese
   Nonstick spray coating
2 tablespoons grated
   Parmesan cheese

● Cook spinach according to package directions, then drain. Squeeze out excess liquid and set aside.

● Meanwhile, in a medium saucepan bring *1½ cups* milk to boiling. Stir together remaining milk and farina. Slowly add farina mixture to boiling milk, stirring constantly. Cook and stir about 3 minutes or till thick. Remove from the heat. Stir about *1 cup* of the hot farina mixture into egg whites, then return all to the saucepan. Stir in ½ cup Parmesan cheese and spinach; mix well.

● Line an 8x8x2-inch baking pan with foil. Pour mixture into the pan. Cover and chill about 1½ hours or until firm. Turn out onto a cutting board. Cut into 4x½-inch rectangles.

● Spray a baking sheet with nonstick coating. Place rectangles on the baking sheet, then sprinkle with 2 tablespoons Parmesan cheese. Bake in a 425° oven for 25 to 30 minutes or until golden. Makes 6 servings.

Breads and Spreads

Oatmeal-Raisin Scones

6 grams fat/serving

A sweet biscuitlike cake that makes a smashing breakfast, brunch, or teatime treat.

1 cup all-purpose flour
3 tablespoons brown sugar
1½ teaspoons baking powder
½ teaspoon ground cinnamon
⅓ cup margarine
1 cup quick-cooking rolled
  oats
½ cup raisins, chopped
2 egg whites
2 tablespoons skim milk
  Skim milk

● Stir together flour, sugar, baking powder, and cinnamon. Cut in margarine till mixture resembles coarse crumbs. Stir in oats and raisins. Add egg whites and 2 tablespoons milk; mix well (dough will be sticky).

● On a lightly floured surface roll or pat dough into a 7-inch circle. Cut into 12 wedges, dipping knife into flour as needed to prevent sticking. Place on an ungreased baking sheet, then brush tops lightly with more milk. Bake in a 400° oven for 10 to 12 minutes or till golden. Serve warm. Makes 12 servings.

Apple-Nut Coffee Bread

4 grams fat/serving

Your morning coffee is built right into this homey breakfast or brunch treat.

1½ cups all-purpose flour
1 teaspoon baking powder
¼ teaspoon baking soda
1¼ cups peeled and shredded
  apple (2 medium)
⅔ cup packed brown sugar
1½ teaspoons instant coffee
  crystals
1 beaten egg
3 tablespoons cooking oil
¼ cup chopped walnuts
  Nonstick spray coating

● Stir together flour, baking powder, and soda, then set aside. In a large bowl combine apple, sugar, and coffee crystals; let stand 5 minutes, stirring once. Add egg and oil; mix well. Stir in flour mixture just till combined. Fold in nuts.

● Spray an 8x4x2-inch loaf pan with nonstick coating, then pour in batter. Bake in a 350° oven about 50 minutes or till a toothpick inserted near the center comes out clean. Cool in the pan for 10 minutes. Remove from pan, then cool thoroughly on a rack. Wrap and store overnight before slicing. Makes 1 loaf or 18 servings.

Apple-Nut Coffee Bread

Oatmeal-Raisin Scones

Orange Sticky Rolls

7 grams fat/serving

Oohey, gooey, and sinlessly delicious! (Pictured on page 39.)

½ cup sugar
2 tablespoons light corn
    syrup
1½ teaspoons finely shredded
    orange peel
2 tablespoons orange juice
1 tablespoon margarine
    Nonstick spray coating
2 cups all-purpose flour
1 tablespoon baking powder
¼ cup margarine
¾ cup skim milk
2 tablespoons sugar
½ teaspoon ground cinnamon

● In a medium saucepan stir together ½ cup sugar, corn syrup, orange peel, orange juice, and 1 tablespoon margarine. Bring just to boiling, stirring constantly. Spray an 8x8x2-inch or a 9x9x2-inch baking pan with nonstick coating. Pour in orange mixture and set aside.

● Stir together flour and baking powder. Cut in ¼ cup margarine till mixture resembles coarse crumbs. Make a well in the center. Add milk, stirring just till dough clings together. Turn out onto a lightly floured surface and knead gently 15 to 20 strokes. Roll into a 12x9-inch rectangle.

● Stir together 2 tablespoons sugar and cinnamon, then sprinkle over dough. Roll up jelly-roll style, starting from one of the short sides. Slice into nine pieces. Place, cut side down, on top of orange mixture in pan. Bake in a 425° oven for 20 to 25 minutes or till golden. Cool 1 minute. Loosen sides, then invert onto a plate. Serve warm. Makes 9 servings.

Cranberry Muffins

6 grams fat/serving

For a fat-free finale, brush baked muffins with orange juice and sprinkle lightly with sugar.

1 cup cranberries, coarsely
    chopped
2 tablespoons sugar
1¾ cups all-purpose flour
¼ cup sugar
1½ teaspoons baking powder
½ teaspoon ground cinnamon
¼ teaspoon salt
2 slightly beaten egg whites
½ cup skim milk
⅓ cup cooking oil
    Nonstick spray coating

● In a small bowl stir together cranberries and 2 tablespoons sugar; set aside.

● Stir together flour, ¼ cup sugar, baking powder, cinnamon, and salt. Make a well in the center. Combine egg whites, milk, oil, and cranberry mixture. Add to dry ingredients, then stir just till moistened (batter should be lumpy).

● Spray muffin cups with nonstick coating, then fill three-fourths full. Bake in a 400° oven for 20 to 25 minutes or until golden. Remove from the pan. Serve warm. Makes 12 muffins.

Apple Orchard Spread

0 grams fat/serving

Reach for this spiced spread instead of butter or margarine.

3 cups sliced, peeled
   apples (3 medium)
⅓ cup water
½ cup packed brown sugar
¼ teaspoon ground cinnamon
⅛ teaspoon ground nutmeg
   Dash ground cloves

● In a medium saucepan combine apples and water. Bring to boiling; reduce the heat. Cover and simmer for 8 to 10 minutes or until tender. *Do not drain.*

● Mash apples slightly, then stir in sugar, cinnamon, nutmeg, and cloves. Bring to boiling; reduce heat. Boil gently, uncovered, about 10 minutes or till thickened, stirring occasionally. Cool. Cover and refrigerate or freeze to store. Makes about 1½ cups or 24 (1-tablespoon) servings.

Cinnamon-Raisin Spread

3 grams fat/serving

Sugar and spice and everything nice.

½ of an 8-ounce package
   Neufchâtel cheese
2 tablespoons chopped raisins
1 tablespoon brown sugar
¼ teaspoon ground cinnamon
   Skim milk

● Soften cheese. In a small bowl stir together cheese, raisins, sugar, and cinnamon. Stir in enough milk to make spreadable (about 2 teaspoons). Cover and refrigerate to store. Makes about ⅔ cup or 10 (1-tablespoon) servings.

All Margarine Is Not Alike

It pays for you to know the difference among types of margarines if you're concerned with fat. In general, the softer the margarine, the less saturated fat it contains. That means liquid squeeze margarines are less saturated than soft tub margarines, which are less saturated than soft stick margarines, which are less saturated than hard stick margarines.

In addition to firmness, look at the label. The first ingredient should be *liquid* vegetable oil, such as corn, safflower, or soybean oil.

The label also can clue you in to the P/S ratio—the ratio of polyunsaturated to saturated fat. Check the "Nutrition information per serving" for grams of fat. Margarine that contains 4 grams of polyunsaturated fat and 2 grams of saturated fat has a P/S ratio of 2 to 1. This means it has twice as much polyunsaturated fat as saturated fat, making it a good choice.

Vegetables and Salads

Garlic-Pepper Potatoes

1 gram fat/serving

To quickly make ¼ cup of chicken broth, stir together ¼ cup of hot water and ¼ teaspoon instant chicken bouillon granules.

2 medium potatoes
¼ cup chicken broth
1 tablespoon grated
    Parmesan cheese
1 tablespoon snipped chives
1 clove garlic, minced
⅛ teaspoon pepper
2 tablespoons plain low-fat
    yogurt

● Scrub potatoes and prick with a fork. Bake in a 425° oven for 40 to 60 minutes or until tender. (*Or,* micro-cook potatoes on 100% power (HIGH) for 6 to 8 minutes.) Cut a lengthwise slice from the top of each potato, then discard skin from slice.

● Place potato portions from the slices in a small bowl. Scoop out insides of potatoes, leaving a ¼-inch shell; reserve shells. Mash potato. Add chicken broth and stir till well combined. Stir in Parmesan, chives, garlic, and pepper.

● Pile potato mixture into reserved shells, then place in a shallow baking dish. Return to the 425° oven and bake about 10 minutes or till heated through. Dollop with yogurt. Serves 2.

Green Bean Casserole

1 gram fat/serving

An easy to tote, potluck prizewinner you'll be proud to serve.

1 9-ounce package frozen
    French-style green beans
1 cup sliced cauliflower
    flowerets
1 cup skim milk
    Nonstick spray coating
¼ cup chopped onion
1 tablespoon cornstarch
¼ cup grated Parmesan cheese
2 tablespoons chopped
    pimiento
½ cup coarsely crushed, bite-
    size wheat, rice, corn,
    or bran squares cereal

● Cook beans according to package directions, then drain, reserving ¼ cup liquid. Cook cauliflower in a small amount of boiling water for 4 to 5 minutes or till crisp-tender; drain. Combine reserved bean liquid and milk. Set aside.

● Spray a large saucepan with nonstick coating. Cook onion in the saucepan till tender. Stir together milk mixture and cornstarch, then add to saucepan. Cook and stir till thickened and bubbly. Stir in beans, cauliflower, Parmesan, and pimiento. Transfer to a 1-quart casserole, then sprinkle with cereal. Bake in a 350° oven about 25 minutes or until bubbly. Serves 6.

Mexican Bean Casserole

Nonstick spray coating
½ cup chopped onion
1 clove garlic, minced
1 16-ounce can tomatoes, cut up
1 15½-ounce can red kidney beans, drained and rinsed
1 15-ounce can garbanzo beans, drained and rinsed
1 4-ounce can chopped green chili peppers, drained
1 teaspoon chili powder
Several dashes bottled hot pepper sauce
2 tablespoons cold water
1 tablespoon all-purpose flour
2 cups water
¾ cup yellow cornmeal

● Spray a large saucepan with nonstick coating. Cook onion and garlic in the saucepan till tender. Stir in tomatoes, kidney beans, garbanzo beans, green chili peppers, chili powder, hot pepper sauce, and ¼ teaspoon *salt*. Bring to boiling; reduce the heat. Stir together 2 tablespoons water and flour, then add to saucepan. Cook and stir till thickened and bubbly. Keep warm.

● In a medium saucepan combine 2 cups water, cornmeal, and ½ teaspoon *salt*. Cook and stir till thick and bubbly.

● Spoon hot bean mixture into a 12x7½x2-inch baking dish. Immediately pipe or spoon cornmeal mixture over bean mixture. Bake in a 375° oven about 25 minutes or till cornmeal topper is light brown. Makes 10 servings.

Piping the cornmeal topper
For a special touch, pipe the cornmeal mixture over the casserole. Carefully spoon the hot cornmeal mixture into a pastry bag fitted with a large open star writing tip.

Fold the bag closed and secure it with your writing hand. Hold the full end of the bag with your other hand. Since the cornmeal mixture is hot, use a pot holder while supporting the bag.

Then, force the hot mixture through the tip by squeezing the end of the bag with your writing hand. Support and guide the writing tip with your other hand to make a lattice design.

Pasta Spinach Salad

Pasta Spinach Salad

3 grams fat/serving

Don't travel to Athens for feta cheese—it's right in your grocer's dairy case.

6 ounces rigatoni *or* cavatelli
2 medium tomatoes, peeled, seeded, and chopped
½ cup crumbled feta cheese (2 ounces)
⅓ cup low-calorie Italian salad dressing
¼ cup sliced green onion
2 tablespoons sliced pitted ripe olives
6 cups torn fresh spinach

● Cook pasta according to package directions, then drain. In a bowl combine pasta, tomatoes, cheese, salad dressing, green onion, and olives. Toss gently to coat. Cover and chill. Arrange spinach on a serving platter; spoon on pasta. Makes 8 servings.

Layered Vegetable Salad

4 grams fat/serving

A make-ahead marvel that tastes as great as the popular high-fat version.

1 medium head lettuce, torn into pieces (6 cups)
1 10-ounce package frozen peas, thawed
2 cups thinly sliced cauliflower flowerets
1 cup shredded carrot
2 cups cherry tomatoes, halved
1 cup shredded mozzarella cheese (4 ounces)
½ cup plain low-fat yogurt
⅓ cup reduced-calorie mayonnaise
2 tablespoons sliced green onion
Paprika

● In a large glass bowl layer *half* of the torn lettuce, the peas, cauliflower, and carrot. Add remaining lettuce and tomato halves; sprinkle with cheese. Stir together yogurt and mayonnaise, then spread over top of salad. Cover and chill several hours or overnight. Sprinkle with green onion and paprika. Toss before serving. Makes 12 servings.

Salad Dressings and Sauces

Peppy Salad Dressing

0 grams fat/serving

Fruit pectin, typically used to thicken jams and jellies, gives dressing body without using oil.

1 tablespoon powdered fruit
pectin
1 teaspoon sugar
⅛ teaspoon dry mustard
⅛ teaspoon pepper
¼ cup water
1 tablespoon vinegar
1 small clove garlic, minced

● Combine pectin, sugar, mustard, and pepper. Stir in water, vinegar, and garlic. Cover and chill for 1 hour. Chill to store two or three days. Makes about ½ cup or 8 (1-tablespoon) servings.

Herbed Salad Dressing: Prepare Peppy Salad Dressing as above, *except* add ⅛ teaspoon dried *basil*, crushed, and ⅛ teaspoon *paprika* to the dry pectin mixture. Continue as directed.

Parmesan Salad Dressing: Prepare Peppy Salad Dressing as above, *except* add 1 tablespoon grated *Parmesan cheese* and ¼ teaspoon dried *oregano,* crushed, to the dry pectin mixture. Continue as directed.

Creamy Onion Dressing: Prepare Peppy Salad Dressing as above, *except* increase the sugar to *1 tablespoon* and stir in ¼ cup sliced *green onion* and ¼ cup plain *low-fat yogurt* with the water. Continue as directed.

Orange-Poppy Seed Dressing

1 gram fat/serving

1 8-ounce container plain
low-fat yogurt
1 tablespoon honey
1 tablespoon frozen orange
juice concentrate, thawed
1 teaspoon poppy seed
1 teaspoon finely shredded
orange peel

● Stir together yogurt, honey, orange juice concentrate, poppy seed, and orange peel. Cover and chill to store. Makes about 1 cup or 16 (1-tablespoon) servings.

Honey-Mustard Dressing

0 grams fat/serving

1 8-ounce container plain
low-fat yogurt
1 tablespoon honey
1 tablespoon Dijon-style
mustard
⅛ teaspoon pepper

● In a small bowl stir together low-fat yogurt, honey, mustard, and pepper. Cover and chill to store. Makes about 1 cup or 16 (1-tablespoon) servings.

Herbed Salad Dressing

Orange-Poppy Seed Dressing

Basic Cheese Sauce

2 grams fat/serving

This smooth sauce and its variations are heavenly on fresh steamed vegetables.

1 tablespoon margarine
4 teaspoons cornstarch
⅛ teaspoon pepper *or* white pepper
1 cup skim milk
¾ cup shredded American *or* process Swiss cheese (3 ounces)

● In a small saucepan melt margarine. Stir in cornstarch and pepper; add milk. Cook and stir till thickened and bubbly, then cook and stir 2 minutes more. Add cheese, stirring to melt. Makes about 1½ cups or 24 (1-tablespoon) servings.

Garlic-Herb Cheese Sauce: Prepare Basic Cheese Sauce as above, *except* cook 1 clove *garlic,* minced; ¼ teaspoon dried *basil,* crushed; and ¼ teaspoon dried *tarragon,* crushed, in the margarine for 1 minute. Continue as directed.

Mexicali Cheese Sauce: Prepare Basic Cheese Sauce as above, *except* stir ½ teaspoon *chili powder* into the margarine. Add 2 tablespoons chopped canned *green chili peppers* with the milk. Continue as directed, using American cheese.

Easy Vegetable-Horseradish Sauce

1 gram fat/serving

This versatile sauce livens up burgers, sandwiches, and salads.

1 10-ounce package frozen deluxe tiny peas
⅓ cup plain low-fat yogurt
⅓ cup reduced-calorie mayonnaise
2 tablespoons skim milk
1 teaspoon dry mustard
1 teaspoon prepared horseradish
¼ teaspoon pepper
1 4-ounce can sliced mushrooms, drained

● Cook peas according to package directions, then drain. Stir together yogurt, mayonnaise, milk, dry mustard, horseradish, and pepper. Stir in peas and mushrooms. Cover and chill before serving. Makes about 2 cups or 16 (2-tablespoon) servings.

Spiced Citrus Sauce

0 grams fat/serving

For the fruit, we suggest fresh or frozen blueberries, strawberries, or peaches.

2 tablespoons sugar
1 tablespoon cornstarch
½ teaspoon finely shredded orange peel
¼ teaspoon ground nutmeg
¼ teaspoon ground ginger
1 cup orange juice
1 cup desired fruit

● In a small saucepan stir together sugar, cornstarch, orange peel, nutmeg, and ginger. Add orange juice. Cook and stir till thickened and bubbly, then cook and stir 2 minutes more. Stir in fruit; heat through. Serve over pancakes, waffles, or ice milk. Makes about 1⅔ cups or 5 (⅓-cup) servings.

	FAT (g)	CHOLESTEROL (mg)	UNSATURATED FAT (g)	CALORIES	PROTEIN (g)	CARBOHYDRATES (g)	SODIUM (mg)	POTASSIUM (mg)	PROTEIN	VITAMIN A	VITAMIN C	THIAMINE	RIBOFLAVIN	NIACIN	CALCIUM	IRON
				Per Serving					Percent USRDA Per Serving							
SIDE DISHES · RICE AND PASTA																
Baked Spinach Gnocchi (p. 53)	3	11	1	143	11	18	160	329	17	77	24	10	22	4	35	43
Vegetable-Bordered Pasta Bake (p. 52)	7	14	3	191	9	25	306	331	14	25	90	16	18	8	20	8
Bulgur-Rice Pilaf (p. 51)	0	0	0	67	2	15	141	96	3	16	4	4	2	4	1	4
Rice Medley and Vegetables (p. 51)	1	1	0	102	3	22	127	131	4	2	43	7	5	8	2	4
Spinach-Herb Fettuccine (p. 53)	2	3	1	36	5	24	101	97	8	1	1	17	10	9	6	5
BREADS AND SPREADS																
Apple-Nut Coffee Bread (p. 54)	4	14	3	115	2	19	38	72	3	1	1	5	3	3	2	4
Apple Orchard Spread (p. 57)	0	0	0	24	0	6	2	31	0	0	0	0	0	0	0	1
Cinnamon-Raisin Spread (p. 57)	3	9	0	38	1	3	46	29	2	3	0	0	1	0	1	1
Cranberry Muffins (p. 56)	6	0	5	154	3	22	95	47	4	0	2	8	6	5	4	3
Oatmeal-Raisin Scones (p. 54)	6	0	4	138	3	19	110	98	4	4	0	8	4	3	4	5
Orange Sticky Rolls (p. 56)	7	0	5	234	4	40	189	68	6	5	4	13	9	8	9	6
VEGETABLES AND SALADS																
Garlic-Pepper Potatoes (p. 58)	1	4	0	163	6	33	92	800	8	2	65	13	7	14	6	6
Green Bean Casserole (p. 58)	1	5	0	66	5	10	56	204	7	8	35	5	10	2	12	4
Layered Vegetable Salad (p. 61)	4	7	2	83	5	8	95	280	8	36	43	9	7	5	11	8
Mexican Bean Casserole (p. 59)	2	0	0	147	7	27	229	406	10	13	28	9	4	5	4	13
Pasta Spinach Salad (p. 61)	3	6	1	121	5	20	205	303	8	72	45	16	10	8	9	12
SALAD DRESSINGS AND SAUCES																
Basic Cheese Sauce (p. 64)	2	3	1	23	1	1	51	18	2	1	0	0	2	0	4	0
Creamy Onion Dressing (p. 62)	0	1	0	11	0	2	4	21	0	1	2	0	1	0	1	0
Easy Vegetable-Horseradish Sauce (p. 64)	1	1	1	16	1	1	13	18	1	1	3	2	1	1	1	1
Honey-Mustard Dressing (p. 62)	0	1	0	16	1	3	20	23	1	0	0	0	2	0	2	0
Mexicali Cheese Sauce (p. 64)	2	3	1	23	1	1	52	26	2	2	2	0	2	0	4	0
Orange-Poppy Seed Dressing (p. 62)	1	1	0	14	0	2	7	30	1	0	4	1	2	0	2	0
Parmesan Salad Dressing (p. 62)	0	1	0	5	0	1	5	5	0	0	0	0	0	0	1	0
Peppy Salad Dressing (p. 62)	0	0	0	3	0	1	0	4	0	0	0	0	0	0	0	0
Spiced Citrus Sauce (p. 64)	0	0	0	58	1	14	1	149	1	2	72	4	2	2	1	2
Thousand Island Dressing (low-fat, p. 88)	0	1	0	7	0	1	40	26	1	1	3	0	1	0	1	0
Thousand Island Dressing (standard, p. 88)	7	24	5	65	1	1	85	21	1	2	2	1	1	0	0	1
Vinaigrette Dressing (low-fat, p. 88)	5	0	4	52	0	1	53	8	0	0	0	0	0	0	0	0
Vinaigrette Dressing (standard, p. 88)	9	0	7	82	0	1	44	7	0	0	0	0	0	0	0	0

DESSERTS
LOW FAT

If you've crossed desserts off your low-fat list, grab your eraser! Sweet endings needn't mean the finish of your diet. On the contrary, our sweet treats will help you stick to a healthy eating plan.

You'll find old favorites such as chocolate cake and lemon bars — tastefully tailored, of course. As always, we offer some new ideas, too — like a fruity flambé and creamy freezer pops. Choosing will be a delicious dilemma!

Chocolate Sheet Cake

5 grams fat/serving

Keep the fat in line by simply dusting the top with powdered sugar.

2 cups all-purpose flour
2 cups sugar
1 teaspoon baking soda
1⅓ cups water
½ cup margarine
⅓ cup unsweetened cocoa
    powder
½ cup buttermilk
2 egg whites
1 egg
1½ teaspoons vanilla

● Lightly grease and flour a 15x10x1-inch baking pan, then set aside. In a large mixer bowl stir together flour, sugar, and soda.

● In a medium saucepan combine water, margarine, and cocoa powder. Bring just to boiling, stirring constantly. Remove from the heat. Add to dry ingredients, beating on low speed of electric mixer just till combined. Add buttermilk, egg whites, egg, and vanilla. Beat on low speed for 1 minute (batter will be thin).

● Pour into the prepared pan. Bake in a 350° oven for 20 to 25 minutes or till a toothpick inserted near the center comes out clean. Cool completely. Makes 20 servings.

Chocolate-Nutmeg Bavarian

3 grams fat/serving

Chill this luscious dessert in a 3-cup bowl if you're short on individual molds.

¼ cup sugar
3 tablespoons unsweetened
    cocoa powder
1 teaspoon unflavored gelatin
⅛ teaspoon ground nutmeg
½ cup evaporated skimmed
    milk
1 egg white
½ teaspoon vanilla
⅛ teaspoon cream of tartar
2 tablespoons sugar
⅓ of an 8-ounce container
    (about 1 cup) frozen
    whipped dessert
    topping, thawed
Nonstick spray coating

● In a medium saucepan stir together ¼ cup sugar, cocoa powder, gelatin, and nutmeg; add milk. Stir over low heat till gelatin dissolves. Remove from the heat, then cover the surface with clear plastic wrap. Chill for 25 to 30 minutes or to the consistency of corn syrup. Remove from the refrigerator (mixture will continue to set).

● Immediately combine egg white, vanilla, and cream of tartar in a small mixer bowl. Beat on medium speed of an electric mixer till soft peaks form (tips curl). Gradually add 2 tablespoons sugar, beating till stiff peaks form (tips stand straight).

● When gelatin mixture is the consistency of unbeaten egg whites (partially set), fold in stiffly beaten egg white and dessert topping. Chill till mixture mounds when spooned. Transfer to six ½-cup molds sprayed with nonstick coating. Cover and chill several hours or till firm. Unmold onto dessert dishes. Garnish with fresh fruit, if desired. Makes 6 servings.

Glazed Fruit Pie

It's important to add the kiwi fruit just before serving. The fruit contains enzymes that can break down the gelatin in the glaze.

¾ cup finely crushed ginger-snaps (12 cookies)
½ cup finely crushed graham crackers (7 crackers)
1 tablespoon sugar
3 tablespoons margarine, melted
1 8-ounce can pineapple slices (juice pack)
Unsweetened pineapple juice
1 envelope unflavored gelatin
2 small bananas
2 cups sliced strawberries
2 kiwi fruit, peeled and sliced

● Stir together gingersnaps, graham crackers, and sugar. Drizzle with margarine, tossing to combine. Press onto bottom and up sides of a 9-inch pie plate to form a firm, even crust. Bake in a 375° oven for 5 minutes. Cool.

● For glaze, drain pineapple, reserving juice. Cut pineapple into small pieces and set aside. Add enough unsweetened pineapple juice (about 1½ cups) to the reserved juice to make 1¾ cups total liquid. In a small saucepan stir together pineapple liquid and gelatin, then let stand 5 minutes. Stir over low heat till gelatin dissolves. Cover and chill to the consistency of unbeaten egg whites (partially set).

● Spread ⅓ cup of the glaze over the bottom of the crust. Slice bananas and arrange over glaze. Top with another ⅓ cup of the glaze and arrange strawberries over glaze. Stir together pineapple pieces and remaining glaze, then spoon over strawberries. Chill for 2 to 4 hours or till set. Before serving, arrange kiwi fruit on pie. Makes 8 servings.

Lemon Bars

Nonstick spray coating
¼ cup margarine
3 tablespoons sugar
¾ cup all-purpose flour
2 slightly beaten egg whites
1 beaten egg
¾ cup sugar
¼ teaspoon finely shredded lemon peel
3 tablespoons lemon juice
2 tablespoons all-purpose flour
¼ teaspoon baking powder

● Spray an 8x8x2-inch baking pan with nonstick coating. In a small mixer bowl beat margarine on medium speed of an electric mixer about 30 seconds. Add 3 tablespoons sugar, then beat till fluffy. Stir in ¾ cup flour. Pat onto the bottom of the pan. Bake in a 350° oven for 15 minutes.

● Meanwhile, in the bowl combine egg whites and egg. Add ¾ cup sugar, lemon peel, lemon juice, 2 tablespoons flour, and baking powder. Beat on medium speed about 3 minutes or till slightly thickened, then pour over baked layer in pan. Continue baking for 25 to 30 minutes or till edges are light brown and center is set. Cool. Sift lightly with powdered sugar, if desired. Cut into bars. Makes 16 servings.

Glazed Fruit Pie

Meringue and Fruit Flambé

3 egg whites
1 teaspoon vanilla
¼ teaspoon cream of tartar
¾ cup sugar
2 tablespoons unsweetened
　　cocoa powder
2 medium oranges
　　Orange juice
1 tablespoon cornstarch
¼ teaspoon ground allspice
1 tablespoon lemon juice
2 small peaches, sliced, *or*
　　one 8-ounce can peach
　　slices (juice pack), drained
1 small banana, sliced
¼ cup raisins
1 quart vanilla ice milk
2 tablespoons brandy

● Cover a baking sheet with brown paper or foil. Draw eight 3-inch circles on paper, then set aside. For meringue shells, in a large mixer bowl beat egg whites, vanilla, and cream of tartar on medium speed of an electric mixer till soft peaks form (tips curl). Gradually add *½ cup* sugar, beating till stiff peaks form (tips stand straight). Stir together remaining sugar and cocoa powder; fold into egg white mixture. Spread over each circle, forming a shell. Bake in a 300° oven for 35 minutes. Turn off oven. Let stand 1 hour in the oven. Cool; remove from paper.

● For sauce, section oranges over a bowl to catch juice. Add enough additional orange juice to make ¾ cup total liquid. Stir together cornstarch and allspice; add orange juice and lemon juice. Cook and stir till thickened and bubbly, then cook and stir 2 minutes more. Stir in fruit and heat through.

● Place one scoop ice milk in each meringue shell. In a small saucepan heat brandy just till hot. Using a long match, ignite brandy. Stir into sauce; ladle over ice milk. Makes 8 servings.

Assembling the dessert
When you shape the meringue shells, be sure to build up the sides with a spoon, making a dip in the center. This makes it easier for the meringues to hold the ice milk.

The meringue shells can be made ahead and stored in a cool, dry place. To serve, place them on individual dessert plates. Put a scoop of ice milk in each shell, then spoon the warm fruit sauce over the ice milk as soon as the flame is out. Serve immediately.

If you're serving this to guests, turn down the lights so they can see the flame when you ignite the brandy.

Chocolate-Peanut Meringue Kisses

2 grams fat/cookie

Kiss your fat worries good-bye.

2 egg whites
½ teaspoon vanilla
½ cup sugar
2 tablespoons unsweetened
  cocoa powder
½ cup coarsely chopped dry
  roasted peanuts
  Nonstick spray coating

● In a large mixer bowl beat egg whites and vanilla on medium speed of an electric mixer till soft peaks form (tips curl). Gradually add *half* of the sugar, beating on medium speed till stiff peaks form (tips stand straight).

● Stir together remaining sugar and cocoa powder; gently fold into beaten egg whites till well combined. Fold in peanuts.

● Spray a cookie sheet with nonstick coating. Drop mixture by slightly rounded tablespoonfuls onto the cookie sheet. Bake in a 325° oven about 20 minutes or till set. Remove from cookie sheet and cool on a wire rack. Makes 24 cookies.

Confetti Oatmeal Drops

2 grams fat/cookie

Wholesome cookies, speckled with carrot and zucchini, that magically disappear.

1½ cups all-purpose flour
 1 teaspoon ground cinnamon
 ¾ teaspoon baking powder
 ¼ teaspoon salt
 ⅓ cup margarine
 ⅔ cup sugar
 1 egg
 ½ teaspoon vanilla
 ½ cup finely shredded
   unpeeled zucchini
 ½ cup finely shredded carrot
 ¾ cup quick-cooking rolled
   oats
 ½ cup raisins

● Stir together flour, cinnamon, baking powder, and salt; set aside. In a large mixer bowl beat margarine on medium speed of an electric mixer about 30 seconds. Add sugar; beat till fluffy. Add egg and vanilla; beat well. Beat in zucchini and carrot.

● Add flour mixture to creamed mixture, beating on low speed till well combined. Stir in oats and raisins.

● Drop by rounded teaspoonfuls about 2 inches apart onto an ungreased cookie sheet. Bake in a 350° oven about 12 minutes or till golden. Remove from the cookie sheet and cool on a wire rack. Makes about 34 cookies.

Peanut Butter-Fruit Crispies

2 grams fat/serving

We've made a little peanut butter go a long way.

¼ cup packed brown sugar
¼ cup light corn syrup
⅓ cup chunk-style peanut
  butter
2 cups crisp rice cereal
¾ cup chopped mixed
  dried fruit

● In a large saucepan stir together sugar and corn syrup. Stir over medium heat till sugar dissolves, then remove from the heat. Add peanut butter; mix well. Stir in cereal and fruit till well coated. Press into an ungreased 8x8x2-inch baking pan. Cool till firm, then cut into bars. Makes 24 servings.

Cherry-Nut Ice Milk

Vanilla Ice Milk

0 grams fat/serving

Some things are still worth that extra homemade effort.

1½ cups sugar
2 envelopes unflavored gelatin
2 12-ounce cans (3 cups) evaporated skimmed milk
2 slightly beaten egg whites
1 beaten egg
5 cups skim milk
4 teaspoons vanilla

● In a large saucepan combine sugar and gelatin. Stir in evaporated milk. Cook and stir over medium-low heat till mixture almost boils and sugar dissolves, then remove from the heat.

● Stir together egg whites and egg. Stir about *1 cup* of the hot mixture into egg mixture; return all to the saucepan. Cook and stir 2 minutes more, then add skim milk and vanilla. Cool. Freeze the mixture in a 4- or 5-quart ice cream freezer according to the manufacturer's directions. Makes about 3 quarts or 24 (½-cup) servings.

Mint-Chocolate Chip Ice Milk: Prepare Vanilla Ice Milk as above, *except* stir in ¼ cup *green crème de menthe* with the vanilla. Stir 3 squares (3 ounces) chopped *semisweet chocolate* into the cooled milk mixture. Continue as directed.

Cherry-Nut Ice Milk: Prepare Vanilla Ice Milk as above, *except* stir 1 cup chopped *walnuts*, 1 cup chopped *maraschino cherries*, and 3 tablespoons *maraschino cherry juice* into the cooled milk mixture. Continue as directed.

Quick Yogurt Pops

1 gram fat/serving

Take your pick! For the fruit, choose peaches, plums, strawberries, or bananas.

2 tablespoons skim milk
1 teaspoon unflavored gelatin
2 8-ounce cartons low-fat vanilla yogurt
2 tablespoons honey
1½ cups chopped fresh *or* canned fruit
10 3-ounce paper cups
10 wooden sticks

● In a medium saucepan stir together milk and gelatin, then let stand 5 minutes. Stir over low heat till gelatin dissolves. Stir in yogurt and honey, then fold in fruit.

● Spoon mixture into paper cups. Cover each cup with a small piece of foil. Cut a slit in the center of the foil, then push a stick through foil and into the mixture.

● Freeze about 5 hours or till the mixture is firm. To serve, let stand at room temperature about 10 minutes, then peel off the cups. Makes 10 servings.

Home-Style Apple-Raisin Crisp

10 grams fat/serving

Tastes just like Mom used to make, with a fraction of the fat.

4	cups thinly sliced, peeled apples
¼	cup raisins
2	teaspoons lemon juice
1	tablespoon brown sugar
½	teaspoon ground cinnamon
¼	teaspoon ground nutmeg
¼	cup quick-cooking rolled oats
2	tablespoons all-purpose flour
1	tablespoon brown sugar
½	teaspoon ground cinnamon
2	tablespoons margarine
1	pint vanilla ice milk

● In a medium bowl combine apples and raisins, then toss with lemon juice. Stir together 1 tablespoon brown sugar, ½ teaspoon cinnamon, and nutmeg; sprinkle over apple mixture. Toss gently to coat. Place in a 1-quart casserole. Cover and bake in a 375° oven for 25 minutes.

● Meanwhile, stir together oats, flour, 1 tablespoon brown sugar, and ½ teaspoon cinnamon. Cut in margarine till mixture resembles coarse crumbs; sprinkle over apple mixture. Return to the oven and bake, uncovered, for 15 to 20 minutes more or till apples are tender. Serve warm with ice milk. Serves 4.

Blueberry Cobbler

6 grams fat/serving

Bubbly berries with a whole-grain topper.

⅓	cup sugar
1	tablespoon cornstarch
¾	cup orange juice
2½	cups fresh *or* frozen blueberries
½	cup all-purpose flour
½	cup whole wheat flour
1½	teaspoons baking powder
⅓	cup skim milk
3	tablespoons cooking oil
1	teaspoon sugar

● In a small saucepan stir together ⅓ cup sugar and cornstarch, then add orange juice. Cook and stir till thickened and bubbly. Add blueberries; cook until berries are hot. Keep warm.

● Stir together flours and baking powder. Add milk and oil; stir until mixture forms a ball. On a lightly floured surface pat into an 8-inch circle, then cut into eight wedges.

● Spoon hot berry mixture into a 9-inch pie plate and immediately top with wedges. Sprinkle with 1 teaspoon sugar. Bake in a 425° oven for 25 to 30 minutes or till wedges are brown. Serve warm. Makes 8 servings.

	FAT (g)	CHOLESTEROL (mg)	UNSATURATED FAT (g)	CALORIES	PROTEIN (g)	CARBOHYDRATES (g)	SODIUM (mg)	POTASSIUM (mg)	PROTEIN	VITAMIN A	VITAMIN C	THIAMINE	RIBOFLAVIN	NIACIN	CALCIUM	IRON
				Per Serving					Percent USRDA Per Serving							
DESSERTS																
Blueberry Cobbler (p. 74)	6	0	4	179	3	31	61	134	4	2	30	9	5	5	6	6
Cherry-Nut Ice Milk (p. 73)	4	13	3	151	6	25	71	212	9	3	2	3	12	1	16	2
Chocolate Cake (low-fat, p. 89)	11	22	7	300	4	49	196	127	6	8	0	9	8	6	3	7
Chocolate Cake (standard, p. 89)	19	60	10	359	4	46	112	116	7	7	1	9	8	6	3	7
Chocolate-Nutmeg Bavarian (p. 67)	3	1	0	114	4	19	34	120	6	2	0	1	5	1	7	2
Chocolate-Peanut Meringue Kisses (p. 71)	2	0	1	36	1	5	17	31	2	0	0	1	1	3	0	1
Chocolate Sheet Cake (p. 67)	5	13	4	174	3	31	127	52	4	4	0	6	5	4	1	3
Confetti Oatmeal Drops (p. 71)	2	7	2	68	1	11	47	39	2	5	1	3	2	2	1	2
Glazed Fruit Pie (p. 68)	6	4	4	196	3	35	151	378	4	6	88	8	7	5	4	8
Home-Style Apple-Raisin Crisp (p. 74)	10	13	6	276	4	46	120	359	7	8	7	7	11	1	12	6
Lemon Bars (p. 68)	3	16	2	103	2	17	50	22	2	3	2	3	3	2	1	2
Meringue and Fruit Flambé (p. 70)	4	13	1	236	6	48	65	360	8	10	34	6	13	3	12	4
Mint-Chocolate Chip Ice Milk (p. 73)	2	13	1	113	6	20	71	208	9	3	2	2	12	1	16	2
Peanut Butter-Fruit Crispies (p. 71)	2	0	1	61	1	11	49	69	2	6	2	2	3	4	1	3
Quick Yogurt Pops (p. 73)	1	4	0	47	2	8	25	123	3	7	4	2	6	2	6	1
Vanilla Ice Milk (p. 73)	0	13	0	98	5	19	71	187	8	3	2	2	12	0	16	1

On any kind of diet, a snack can mean disaster. But our fat-fighting philosophy is: If you can't beat the munchies, join 'em — as long as you choose our fat-reduced versions. How much you eat or drink between meals still counts in the overall scheme of low-fat eating, so pay attention to our serving sizes.

Treat yourself to our snack-size pizza wedges, pâté, spreads, and dip. Or slurp down a thick shake or a mug of steaming-hot cocoa.

Pita Pizza Wedges

3 grams fat/serving

A hearty snack to soothe the savage stomach growl.

2 6½-inch pita bread rounds
½ cup pizza sauce
1 4-ounce can chopped mushrooms, drained
½ cup shredded mozzarella cheese (2 ounces)

● Split each pita round in half horizontally. Quarter each round, forming 16 triangles total. Place on a baking sheet. Bake in a 325° oven for 18 to 20 minutes or till crisp and golden.

● Spread pizza sauce over toasted triangles. Top with mushrooms and cheese. Return to oven and bake about 5 minutes more or till cheese melts. Makes 4 servings.

Parmesan Mushroom Caps

2 grams fat/serving

Save the mushroom stems to toss into your favorite salad.

20 large fresh mushrooms (2- to 2½-inch diameter)
½ of an 8-ounce package Neufchâtel cheese, softened
½ teaspoon Worcestershire sauce
Dash garlic powder
Dash bottled hot pepper sauce
¼ cup finely shredded carrot
¼ cup finely chopped green onion
3 tablespoons grated Parmesan cheese

● Remove stems from mushrooms (save for another use). Simmer mushroom caps in a small amount of water for 2 minutes. Drain, then invert caps on paper towels. Cool.

● In a small mixing bowl stir together Neufchâtel cheese, Worcestershire sauce, garlic powder, and hot pepper sauce. Stir in carrot, onion, and Parmesan. Spoon into mushroom caps, then place in a shallow baking dish. Bake in a 350° oven about 15 minutes or till heated through. Makes 20 servings.

Marinated Vegetable Appetizer

6 grams fat/serving

Yellow summer squash makes a great stand-in for zucchini.

2 cups fresh mushrooms
1 medium zucchini, cut into bite-size chunks
⅓ cup white wine vinegar
¼ cup cooking oil
1 tablespoon dry sherry
1 teaspoon sugar
¼ teaspoon dried oregano, crushed
Dash pepper

● Halve any large mushrooms. In a medium mixing bowl combine mushrooms and zucchini.

● In a screw-top jar combine vinegar, oil, sherry, sugar, oregano, and pepper. Cover and shake well to mix, then pour over vegetables. Cover and chill several hours, stirring occasionally. To serve, drain vegetables and arrange on a serving platter. Makes 4 servings.

Curried Cheese Spread

½ cup finely shredded carrot
2 tablespoons finely chopped
    onion
2 tablespoons snipped parsley
1 tablespoon grated
    Parmesan cheese
½ teaspoon curry powder
1 8-ounce package Neufchâtel
    cheese, softened
½ cup snipped alfalfa sprouts
¼ cup shredded carrot

● In a small mixing bowl stir together ½ cup carrot, onion, parsley, Parmesan, and curry powder. Add Neufchâtel cheese and stir till well combined.

● Transfer to a serving bowl, then sprinkle with alfalfa sprouts and ¼ cup carrot. Cover and chill to store. Makes about 1⅓ cups or 21 (1-tablespoon) servings.

For easy spreading, choose sturdy vegetables such as celery stalks, cucumber rounds, whole radishes, and zucchini sticks. Melba toast rounds or squares make good choices, too. They provide a crunchy contrast to the creamy spread.

Herb-Garlic Spread

3 grams fat/serving

¼ cup chopped green onion
2 tablespoons snipped parsley
1 clove garlic, minced
½ teaspoon dried basil, crushed
1 8-ounce package Neufchâtel cheese, softened
2 tablespoons skim milk

● Combine onion, parsley, garlic, basil, and ⅛ teaspoon *pepper*. Add cheese and milk, then stir till well combined.

● Cover and chill the mixture to store. Makes about 1¼ cups or 20 (1-tablespoon) servings.

Poultry Pâté

1 gram fat/serving

This one's a winner—we backed down on high-cholesterol liver and used lean ground turkey.

¾ pound frozen ground raw turkey, thawed
½ cup chopped onion
2 cloves garlic, minced
¼ pound chicken livers, cut up
¾ cup skim milk
2 egg whites
2 tablespoons fine dry bread crumbs
½ teaspoon ground sage
¼ teaspoon salt
¼ teaspoon pepper
Nonstick spray coating

● Cook turkey, onion, and garlic till meat is brown and onion is tender. Add liver. Cook and stir over medium-high heat about 3 minutes or till liver is no longer pink. Cool about 5 minutes.

● In a blender container place turkey mixture and milk. Cover and blend well. Add egg whites, bread crumbs, cornstarch, sage, salt, and pepper. Cover and blend till well combined.

● Spray a 7½x3½x2-inch loaf pan with nonstick coating. Spoon mixture into pan. Cover with foil; place in a shallow pan. Pour hot water around loaf pan to a depth of ½ inch.

● Bake in a 325° oven 1 hour or until a knife inserted near center comes out clean. Cool; cover and chill. To serve, unmold onto a serving plate. Makes 2½ cups or 40 (1-tablespoon) servings.

Spreadable Edibles

Fresh vegetables and low-fat crackers and breads make fitting accompaniments for our fat-reduced spreads and dip. Vegetable options include carrot, celery, and zucchini sticks; green pepper strips; mushrooms; and broccoli and cauliflower flowerets. Instead of high-fat crackers and chips, choose melba toast, breadsticks, or quartered pita bread rounds.

Fat totals with each recipe and the nutrition analysis on page 83 are figured only for the spreads and dip.

Chunky Chili Dip

1 gram fat/serving

Take a dip with carrot sticks, celery sticks, cauliflower flowerets, or green onions.

⅔ cup plain low-fat yogurt
⅓ cup reduced-calorie
    mayonnaise
¼ cup finely chopped green
    pepper
¼ cup chili sauce
2 tablespoons finely chopped
    green onion
1 tablespoon prepared
    horseradish

● In a mixing bowl stir together yogurt, mayonnaise, green pepper, chili sauce, onion, and horseradish. Cover and chill to store. Makes about 1½ cups or 24 (1-tablespoon) servings.

Wonton Chips

3 grams fat/serving

Our Editors rated these crunchy baked wonton skins outstanding!

12 wonton skins
2 teaspoons margarine,
    melted
    Nonstick spray coating
2 tablespoons grated
    Parmesan cheese
¼ teaspoon dried basil,
    crushed

● Brush wonton skins lightly on one side with margarine. Cut in half diagonally, forming 24 triangles. Spray a 15x10x1-inch baking pan with nonstick coating.

● Arrange triangles in a single layer in the pan, margarine side up. Sprinkle with cheese and basil. Bake in a 400° oven about 7 minutes or till golden brown and crisp. Makes 4 servings.

Creamy Straw-Bana Shakes

1 gram fat/serving

For a fruity frozen treat, freeze the blended mixture in a bowl. Then, let the frozen mixture stand about 30 minutes and scrape the surface with a spoon, forming a slush.

2 ripe medium bananas
1¼ cups skim milk
1 10-ounce package frozen
    strawberries, slightly
    thawed
½ cup low-fat cottage cheese
5 large ice cubes

● Peel and cut up bananas. Wrap in foil, then freeze about 1 hour or till firm. In a blender container combine bananas, milk, berries, and cottage cheese. Cover and blend till smooth. Add ice cubes, then cover and blend till smooth. Garnish each glass with a fresh strawberry, if desired. Makes 4 (8-ounce) servings.

Orange-Buttermilk Nog
(see recipe, page 82)

Creamy Straw-Bana Shakes

Low-Fat Dairy Choices

Warning: Some dairy products can easily sabotage a low-fat life-style. Fight back by choosing cheeses, milk, and dessert products that are low in total fat.

Start by substituting low-fat milk for whole milk, and eventually work your way to skim. Don't forget buttermilk—it's as low in fat as skim milk. Pour yourself a glass for a tangy taste treat.

Even an all-around favorite such as cheese can be enjoyed without guilt. Low-fat cottage cheese is our first pick over cream-style cottage cheese, and mozzarella is lower in fat than other hard cheeses, such as cheddar and Swiss. Buy the low-moisture, part-skim variety of mozzarella cheese. Check the dairy case for specially made low-fat versions of cheddar and other hard cheeses. Neufchâtel cheese makes a great stand-in for cream cheese in dips or spreads, without sacrificing richness.

Ice milk before ice cream is good advice to remember. It satisfies a sweet craving with less fat. If you must spoon it on, remember that nondairy dessert toppings are lower in fat and cholesterol than dairy whipped cream.

Orange-Buttermilk Nog

0 grams fat/serving

An eggless nog, special enough for any occasion. (Pictured on page 81.)

3 cups buttermilk
1 6-ounce can frozen orange juice concentrate
3 tablespoons brown sugar
1 teaspoon vanilla
4 large ice cubes

● In a blender container combine buttermilk, frozen orange juice concentrate, sugar, and vanilla. Cover and blend till smooth. Add ice cubes, then cover and blend till smooth and frothy. Garnish each serving with a mint sprig and an orange twist, if desired. Makes about 6 (6-ounce) servings.

Banana Smoothie

1 gram fat/serving

We don't monkey around when it comes to reducing fat deliciously!

1 ripe large banana
1½ cups skim milk
1 8-ounce carton low-fat vanilla yogurt
¼ cup sifted powdered sugar
3 or 4 large ice cubes
Ground nutmeg

● Cut banana into chunks. In a blender container combine banana, milk, yogurt, and sugar. Cover and blend till smooth. Add ice cubes, then cover and blend till smooth. Sprinkle each serving with nutmeg. Makes 4 (7-ounce) servings.

Spiced Cocoa Mix

For a thoughtful touch, offer coffee liqueur and a cinnamon stick with each serving.

2 cups nonfat dry milk powder
½ cup powdered nondairy creamer
⅓ cup sifted powdered sugar
¼ cup unsweetened cocoa powder
¾ teaspoon ground cinnamon
½ teaspoon ground nutmeg

● For cocoa mix, stir together milk powder, nondairy creamer, sugar, cocoa powder, cinnamon, and nutmeg. Cover and store in an airtight container.

● For each serving, in a heat-proof mug add ¾ cup *boiling water* to ⅛ *cup* cocoa mix, then stir to dissolve. Makes 2⅔ cups mix or enough for 8 (6-ounce) servings.

NUTRITION · ANALYSIS

	FAT (g)	CHOLESTEROL (mg)	UNSATURATED FAT (g)	CALORIES	PROTEIN (g)	CARBOHYDRATES (g)	SODIUM (mg)	POTASSIUM (mg)	PROTEIN	VITAMIN A	VITAMIN C	THIAMINE	RIBOFLAVIN	NIACIN	CALCIUM	IRON
				Per Serving					Percent USRDA Per Serving							
SNACKS AND BEVERAGES																
Banana Smoothie (p. 82)	1	6	0	114	6	21	77	340	9	2	8	5	17	2	18	1
Chunky Chili Dip (p. 80)	1	2	1	15	0	1	42	24	0	1	4	0	1	0	1	0
Creamy Straw-Bana Shakes (p. 80)	1	4	0	181	8	38	156	438	12	3	74	5	16	4	13	5
Curried Cheese Spread (p. 78)	3	9	0	32	1	1	46	23	2	9	1	0	2	0	1	1
Herb-Garlic Spread (p. 79)	3	9	0	31	1	1	46	21	2	4	2	0	2	0	1	0
Marinated Vegetable Appetizer (p. 77)	9	0	7	80	1	5	6	244	2	2	14	4	11	9	1	3
Orange-Buttermilk Nog (p. 82)	0	3	0	121	5	25	161	437	8	6	102	11	14	3	17	2
Parmesan Mushroom Caps (p. 77)	2	5	0	23	1	1	33	74	2	5	2	1	5	3	1	1
Pita Pizza Wedges (p. 77)	3	8	1	110	6	13	268	14	10	2	0	4	8	4	13	5
Poultry Pâté (p. 79)	1	29	0	26	4	1	34	49	6	7	1	1	6	5	1	2
Spiced Cocoa Mix (p. 83)	1	4	0	97	7	15	90	334	10	0	2	4	19	1	22	2
Swedish Meatballs (low-fat, p. 85)	1	8	1	27	3	1	47	39	4	1	1	1	2	3	1	2
Swedish Meatballs (standard, p. 85)	4	18	1	46	2	1	73	31	4	2	0	1	2	2	1	2
Wonton Chips (p. 80)	3	3	2	73	2	10	95	16	2	1	0	3	2	2	2	1

Here's where the fat-skimming principles we've been touting really pay off. We'd like to introduce you to our special recipe blueprints. They're designed to show how you can slash the fat from your own recipes.

Check out our defatted recipes for meatballs, lasagna, stroganoff, salad dressings, and chocolate cake. With subtle changes in ingredients and recipe preparation, you'll see how simple fat-trimming can be.

Swedish Meatballs

½ cup chopped onion
3 tablespoons butter *or*
   margarine
1 beaten egg
1 cup light cream
1½ cups soft bread crumbs
¼ cup finely snipped parsley
½ teaspoon salt
   Dash ground nutmeg
   Dash ground ginger
   Dash pepper
1½ pounds ground beef
2 tablespoons all-purpose
   flour
1 teaspoon instant beef
   bouillon granules
1¼ cups water

Cook onion in *1 tablespoon* of the butter or margarine till tender. In a medium mixing bowl combine egg and cream. Stir in onion, crumbs, parsley, salt, nutmeg, ginger, and pepper. Add beef and mix well. Chill. Shape mixture into 1-inch meatballs.

In a large skillet brown meatballs, half at a time, in the remaining 2 tablespoons butter or margarine. Using a slotted spoon, transfer meatballs to paper towels to drain.

Stir flour and bouillon granules into pan drippings; add water. Cook and stir till thickened and bubbly. Return meatballs to skillet. Cover and simmer about 30 minutes or till the meatballs are done, basting occasionally. Keep warm; serve with toothpicks. Makes 60 appetizer meatballs.

½ cup chopped onion
1 slightly beaten egg white
1 cup skim milk
1½ cups soft bread crumbs
¼ cup finely snipped parsley
½ teaspoon salt
   Dash ground nutmeg
   Dash ground ginger
   Dash pepper
1½ pounds lean ground beef
1 tablespoon margarine
1 tablespoon cornstarch
1½ teaspoons instant beef
   bouillon granules
1½ cups water

Cook onion in a small amount of boiling water about 5 minutes or till tender, then drain. In a medium mixing bowl combine egg white and milk. Stir in onion, crumbs, parsley, salt, nutmeg, ginger, and pepper. Add beef and mix well. Chill. Shape mixture into 1-inch meatballs.

Place meatballs on a rack in a 15x10x1-inch baking pan. Bake in a 375° oven for 15 to 20 minutes or till done. Transfer the meatballs to paper towels to drain well.

In a large skillet melt margarine, then stir in cornstarch and bouillon granules. Add water all at once. Cook and stir till thickened and bubbly, then cook and stir 2 minutes more. Return meatballs to skillet and heat through. Keep warm; serve with toothpicks. Makes 60 appetizer meatballs.

Whenever you run across a recipe step that calls for browning meatballs in butter or other fat, ignore it! That's what we did in this recipe. Ground meat has plenty of its own fat—there's no need to add to it. Instead, switch to lean ground beef and cook the meatballs on a rack in a baking pan so most of the fat drains away.

Other fat-sparing tricks for this recipe include: cooking onion in water instead of butter, using an egg white in place of an egg, and substituting skim milk for cream.

(For complete nutrition analysis, see page 83.)

Lasagna

33 GRAMS FAT/SERVING	12 GRAMS FAT/SERVING

1 pound bulk pork sausage	1 pound lean ground beef
½ cup chopped onion	1 cup chopped onion
1 clove garlic, minced	2 cloves garlic, minced
1 16-ounce can tomatoes, cut up	1 16-ounce can tomatoes, cut up
1 8-ounce can tomato sauce	1 8-ounce can tomato sauce
1 6-ounce can tomato paste	1 6-ounce can tomato paste
2 teaspoons dried basil, crushed	2 teaspoons dried basil, crushed
8 ounces lasagna noodles	1 teaspoon dried oregano, crushed
2 beaten eggs	1 teaspoon fennel seed, crushed
2½ cups ricotta *or* cream-style cottage cheese, drained	⅛ teaspoon ground red pepper
¾ cup grated Parmesan cheese	8 ounces lasagna noodles
1 tablespoon dried parsley flakes	1 beaten egg
½ teaspoon pepper	2 cups low-fat cottage cheese
1 pound mozzarella cheese, sliced	¾ cup grated Parmesan cheese
	1 tablespoon dried parsley flakes
	½ teaspoon pepper
	8 ounces mozzarella cheese (low moisture, part skim milk), sliced

In a large skillet cook meat, onion, and garlic till meat is brown and onion is tender. Drain off fat. Stir in the *undrained* tomatoes, tomato sauce, tomato paste, and basil. Bring to boiling; reduce heat. Cover and simmer for 15 minutes, stirring often.

Meanwhile, cook noodles according to package directions. Drain. Stir together eggs, ricotta or cream-style cottage cheese, ½ cup of the Parmesan, parsley, and pepper.

In a 13x9x2-inch baking dish layer *half* of the noodles, *half* of the ricotta mixture, *half* of the mozzarella, and *half* of the meat sauce. Repeat layers; sprinkle with remaining Parmesan. Bake in a 375° oven for 30 to 35 minutes or till heated through. Let stand for 10 minutes. Serves 10.

In a large skillet cook meat, onion, and garlic till meat is brown and onion is tender. Drain off fat. Stir in the next seven ingredients. Cover; simmer for 15 minutes, stirring often.

Meanwhile, cook noodles according to package directions, *except* omit oil. Drain. Stir together egg, cottage cheese, ½ cup of the Parmesan, parsley, and pepper.

In a 13x9x2-inch baking dish layer *half* of the noodles, *half* of the cottage cheese mixture, *half* of the mozzarella, and *half* of the meat sauce. Repeat layers; sprinkle with remaining Parmesan. Bake in a 375° oven for 30 to 35 minutes or till heated through. Let stand for 10 minutes. Serves 10.

It's easy to transform lean ground beef into a full-flavored substitute for pork sausage. The right sprinkling of herbs and spices, such as oregano, fennel seed, and pepper, give the ground beef a characteristic sausage flavor.

Also, notice the mozzarella cheese. Besides switching to a skim-milk version, we slashed the amount. And the lasagna still tastes rich and cheesy.

Other lean reworks included cutting the amount of eggs in half and using low-fat cottage cheese to replace whole milk ricotta or cream-style cottage cheese.

(For complete nutrition analysis, see page 49.)

Beef Stroganoff

- 1 pound beef tenderloin
- 1 tablespoon all-purpose flour
- 2 tablespoons butter *or* margarine
- 1½ cups sliced fresh mushrooms
- ½ cup chopped onion
- 1 clove garlic, minced
- 2 tablespoons butter *or* margarine
- 1 tablespoon all-purpose flour
- 1¼ cups water
- 1 tablespoon tomato paste
- 1 teaspoon instant beef bouillon granules
- 1 8-ounce carton dairy sour cream
- 2 tablespoons all-purpose flour
- 2 tablespoons dry white wine
- 4 ounces hot cooked noodles

Partially freeze meat, then cut on the bias into thin bite-size strips. Coat meat with 1 tablespoon flour. In a large skillet brown meat in 2 tablespoons butter or margarine. Stir in mushrooms, onion, and garlic, then cook for 3 to 4 minutes or till onion is tender, stirring occasionally. Remove meat-mushroom mixture.

Add 2 tablespoons butter or margarine to pan drippings, then stir in 1 tablespoon flour. Stir in water, tomato paste, and beef bouillon granules. Cook and stir till thickened and bubbly.

In a small bowl stir together sour cream and 2 tablespoons flour; add to skillet. Return meat-mushroom mixture to skillet. Cook and stir till thickened and bubbly, then cook and stir 1 minute more. Stir in wine. Serve over noodles. Makes 4 servings.

- 1 pound beef top round steak
- 1 tablespoon all-purpose flour
- Nonstick spray coating
- 1½ cups sliced fresh mushrooms
- ½ cup chopped onion
- 1 clove garlic, minced
- 1 tablespoon margarine
- 1 tablespoon all-purpose flour
- 1¼ cups water
- 1 tablespoon tomato paste
- 1 teaspoon instant beef bouillon granules
- 1 8-ounce carton plain low-fat yogurt
- 2 tablespoons all-purpose flour
- 2 tablespoons dry white wine
- 4 ounces hot cooked fettuccine

Partially freeze meat, then cut on the bias into thin bite-size strips. Coat meat with 1 tablespoon flour. Spray a large skillet with nonstick coating. Brown meat in skillet. Stir in mushrooms, onion, and garlic, then cook for 3 to 4 minutes or till onion is tender, stirring the mixture occasionally. Remove meat-mushroom mixture.

Add margarine to pan drippings, then stir in 1 tablespoon flour. Stir in water, tomato paste, and bouillon granules. Cook and stir till thickened and bubbly.

Stir together yogurt and 2 tablespoons flour; add to skillet. Return meat-mushroom mixture to skillet. Cook and stir till thickened and bubbly, then cook and stir 1 minute more. Stir in wine. Serve over fettuccine. Makes 4 servings.

Switch from egg noodles to fettuccine or other pasta (they're egg-free) and you save more than 50 percent on fat and even more on cholesterol. And when you cook the pasta, don't put oil in the water. Some oil clings to the pasta after draining, adding unwanted fat. Other fat-cutting tactics include choosing lean meat, cooking with nonstick spray coating instead of butter, and using low-fat yogurt in place of sour cream.

(For complete nutrition analysis, see page 48.)

Thousand Island Dressing

7 GRAMS FAT/SERVING

1 cup mayonnaise
¼ cup chili sauce
2 hard-cooked eggs, chopped
2 tablespoons chopped green pepper
2 tablespoons chopped celery
2 tablespoons chopped onion
1 teaspoon paprika

In a small mixing bowl stir together mayonnaise, chili sauce, eggs, green pepper, celery, onion, and paprika. Cover and chill to store. Makes about 1¾ cups or 28 (1-tablespoon) servings.

0 GRAMS FAT/SERVING

¾ cup plain low-fat yogurt
¼ cup reduced-calorie mayonnaise
¼ cup chili sauce
2 tablespoons chopped green pepper
2 tablespoons chopped celery
2 tablespoons chopped onion
2 tablespoons skim milk
1 teaspoon paprika

In a small mixing bowl stir together yogurt, mayonnaise, chili sauce, green pepper, celery, onion, milk, and paprika. Cover and chill to store. Makes about 1⅔ cups or 26 (1-tablespoon) servings.

Vinaigrette Dressing

9 GRAMS FAT/SERVING

1 cup salad oil
⅔ cup vinegar
1 to 2 teaspoons sugar
1½ teaspoons paprika
½ teaspoon salt
½ teaspoon dried basil, crushed

In a screw-top jar combine all ingredients. Cover and shake well, then chill. Shake again just before serving. Makes about 1½ cups or 24 (1-tablespoon) servings.

5 GRAMS FAT/SERVING

⅔ cup vinegar
½ cup salad oil
2 tablespoons water
1 tablespoon sugar
1½ teaspoons paprika
½ teaspoon salt
½ teaspoon dried basil, crushed

In a screw-top jar combine all ingredients. Cover and shake well, then chill. Shake again just before serving. Makes about 1¼ cups or 20 (1-tablespoon) servings.

A salad dressing can easily destroy the good intentions of a healthy tossed salad. That's why the Thousand Island Dressing starts with a low-fat base of yogurt and reduced-calorie mayonnaise. Then you can pile on the flavor. But don't bother with the eggs—there's so much flavor, they won't be missed.

(For complete nutrition analyses, see page 65.)

Most oil and vinegar recipes boast a lot more oil than vinegar, but that's nothing to brag about for fat watchers. So we reworked the Vinaigrette Dressing to reward you with a full-flavored dressing that's delightfully lean and refreshing. To cut tartness from the vinegar, we added more sugar and water.

Chocolate Cake

1¾ cups all-purpose flour
1 teaspoon baking soda
½ cup shortening
1½ cups sugar
½ teaspoon vanilla
2 eggs
½ cup dairy sour cream
3 squares (3 ounces) unsweetened
  chocolate, melted and cooled
1 cup cold water
¼ cup seedless red raspberry preserves
½ cup whipping cream

Grease and flour two 8x1½-inch or 9x1½-inch round baking pans. Stir together flour and baking soda. In a large mixer bowl beat shortening on medium speed of electric mixer about 30 seconds. Add sugar and vanilla and beat till well combined. Add eggs, one at a time, beating 1 minute after each.

Stir in sour cream and chocolate. Add dry ingredients and cold water alternately to beaten mixture, beating on low speed after each addition just till combined.

Pour batter into baking pans. Bake in a 350° oven for 25 to 30 minutes for 9-inch layers or 30 to 35 minutes for 8-inch layers or till a wooden toothpick inserted near the center comes out clean. Cool 10 minutes on wire racks, then remove from pans. Cool. Whip cream to stiff peaks. To assemble, fill with preserves, then frost top with whipped cream. Makes 12 servings.

1¾ cups all-purpose flour
¾ cup unsweetened cocoa powder
1 teaspoon baking soda
½ cup margarine
1½ cups sugar
½ teaspoon vanilla
1 egg
1 egg white
½ cup plain low-fat yogurt
1 cup cold water
¼ cup seedless red raspberry preserves
1 4-ounce container frozen whipped
  dessert topping, thawed

Lightly grease and flour two 8x1½-inch or 9x1½-inch round baking pans. Stir together flour, cocoa powder, and baking soda. In a large mixer bowl beat margarine on medium speed of electric mixer about 30 seconds. Add sugar and vanilla and beat till well combined. Add egg and egg white, one at a time, beating 1 minute after each.

Stir in yogurt. Add dry ingredients and cold water alternately to beaten mixture, beating on low speed after each addition just till combined.

Pour batter into baking pans. Bake in a 350° oven for 25 to 30 minutes for 9-inch layers or 30 to 35 minutes for 8-inch layers or till a wooden toothpick inserted near the center comes out clean. Cool 10 minutes on wire racks, then remove from pans. Cool. To assemble, fill with preserves, then frost top with dessert topping. Makes 12 servings.

Changing cake formulas is tricky. Though it took some experimenting to get a good quality low-fat cake, here's proof that it can be done! The big switch here was substituting fat-free unsweetened cocoa powder for the chocolate, which contains saturated fat. Using margarine in place of the shortening helped reduce the amount of saturated fat even further.

Other alterations included using one egg and one egg white instead of two whole eggs, substituting yogurt for the sour cream, and frosting with dessert topping rather than whipped cream.

(For complete nutrition analysis, see page 75.)

A—B

FAT (g)		CHOLESTEROL (mg)
1	**APPLE BUTTER;** 1 tablespoon	0
1	**APPLES,** fresh; 1 medium	0
0	**APRICOTS,** fresh; 3 medium	0
0	**ARTICHOKE HEARTS,** frozen; 3½ ounces	0
0	**ASPARAGUS,** cooked; 4 medium spears	0
19	**AVOCADOS,** peeled; ½ avocado	0
0	**BAKING POWDER;** 1 teaspoon	0
0	**BAKING SODA;** 1 teaspoon	0
0	**BANANAS;** 1 medium	0
4	**BARBECUE SAUCE,** bottled; ¼ cup	0
	BEANS	
3	baked, with tomato sauce and pork, canned; ½ cup	5
6	garbanzo, cooked; 1 cup	0
0	green snap, cooked; ½ cup	0
1	kidney, red, canned; 1 cup	0
1	lima, cooked; 1 cup	0
0	**BEAN SPROUTS,** fresh; ½ cup	0
	BEEF	
7	beef for stew, lean only, cooked cubes; ½ cup	102
26	corned, cooked; 3 ounces	80
6	flank steak, cooked, lean only; 3 ounces	80
10	ground beef, cooked, 10% fat; 3 ounces	80
17	ground beef, cooked, 21% fat; 3 ounces	80
9	liver, fried; 3 ounces	372
11	rib roast, cooked, lean only; 3 ounces	77
5	round steak, cooked, lean only; 3 ounces	77
8	rump roast, cooked, lean only; 3 ounces	78
24	short ribs, cooked, lean only; 2½ ounces	51
6	sirloin steak, cooked, lean only; 3 ounces	77
9	T-bone steak, cooked, lean only; 3 ounces	78
8	tenderloin, broiled; ¼ pound raw	47
0	**BEETS,** cooked, sliced; ½ cup	0
	BEVERAGES, alcoholic	
0	beer; 12 ounces	0
0	dessert wine; 1 ounce	0
0	gin, rum, vodka, or whiskey; 1 ounce	0
0	table wine; 1 ounce	0
	BEVERAGES, nonalcoholic	
0	club soda; 8 ounces	0
1	cocoa mix; 1 teaspoon	2
0	coffee, cola, or tea; 8 ounces	0
3	**BISCUITS,** baked from mix; 1 (2-inch diameter)	0
1	**BLACKBERRIES,** fresh or frozen; ½ cup	0
0	**BLUEBERRIES,** fresh or frozen; ½ cup	0
0	**BOUILLON,** instant granules; 1 teaspoon	2

A—B (continued)

FAT (g)		CHOLESTEROL (mg)
	BREAD (see also Rolls)	
5	corn bread; 1 piece (2½x2½x1½ inches)	61
1	crumbs, dry; ¼ cup	1
0	crumbs, soft; ¼ cup	0
0	French; 1 slice (2½x2x½ inches)	0
0	pita; 1 pocket	0
1	raisin; 1 slice	1
0	rye; 1 slice	0
1	white; 1 slice	1
1	whole wheat; 1 slice	1
0	**BROCCOLI,** cooked; 2 medium spears	0
0	**BRUSSELS SPROUTS,** cooked; ½ cup	0
12	**BUTTER,** regular; 1 tablespoon	36

C

FAT (g)		CHOLESTEROL (mg)
0	**CABBAGE,** raw, shredded; 1 cup	0
	CAKES, baked from home recipes	
0	angel, no icing; 1/12 cake	0
13	chocolate, 2 layers, chocolate icing; 1/12 cake	37
4	sponge, no icing; 1/12 cake	155
13	white, uncooked white icing; 1/12 cake	8
13	yellow, chocolate icing; 1/12 cake	42
	CANDY	
3	caramels; 1 ounce (3 medium)	1
5	chocolate fudge; 1 piece (1 ounce)	1
3	peanut brittle; 1 ounce	0
0	**CANTALOUPE;** ¼ medium	0
0	**CARROTS,** raw; 1 medium	0
0	**CATSUP;** 1 tablespoon	0
0	**CAULIFLOWER,** cooked; ½ cup	0
0	**CELERY,** raw; 1 stalk	0
	CEREALS, cooked	
1	oatmeal; ½ cup	0
0	wheat, rolled; ½ cup	0
	CEREALS, ready-to-eat	
0	bite-size shredded wheat biscuits; ½ cup	0
0	bran flakes; ½ cup	0
0	cornflakes; ½ cup	0
4	granola; ¼ cup	0
0	rice, crisp cereal; ½ cup	0
0	wheat flakes; ½ cup	0
	CHEESE	
9	American; 1 ounce	26
9	blue; 1 ounce	25
8	Brie; 1 ounce	28
9	cheddar; 1 ounce	28
5	cottage, cream-style; ½ cup	22

C (continued)

FAT (g)		CHOLESTEROL (mg)
	CHEESE *(continued)*	
0	cottage, dry; ½ cup	5
2	cottage, low-fat; ½ cup	10
11	cream cheese; 1 ounce	31
0	farmer; 1 ounce	2
6	feta; 1 ounce	25
9	Monterey Jack; 1 ounce	28
5	mozzarella, part skim milk; 1 ounce	15
6	mozzarella, whole milk; 1 ounce	22
7	Neufchâtel; 1 ounce	22
1	Parmesan, grated; 1 tablespoon	5
10	ricotta, part skim milk; ½ cup	38
16	ricotta, whole milk; ½ cup	62
6	spread, American; 1 ounce	18
8	Swiss, natural; 1 ounce	28
0	**CHERRIES,** fresh, whole; 10 cherries	0
	CHICKEN	
10	broiler, broiled with skin; 4 ounces	67
6	dark meat, skinned, roasted; 4 ounces	56
15	fryer, batter-fried with skin; 4 ounces	77
3	light meat, skinned, roasted; 4 ounces	56
9	roaster, roasted with skin; 4 ounces	70
8	**CHICKEN LIVERS,** cooked, chopped; 1 cup	883
0	**CHILI POWDER;** 1 teaspoon	0
	CHOCOLATE	
9	milk, plain; 1 ounce	6
10	semisweet; 1 ounce	0
3	syrup, fudge-type; 1 tablespoon	0
0	syrup, thin-type; 1 tablespoon	0
15	unsweetened; 1 ounce	0
	CLAMS, raw	
1	hard; 3 ounces	43
2	soft; 3 ounces	43
1	**COCOA POWDER,** unsweetened; 1 tablespoon	0
14	**COCONUT,** fresh, shredded; ½ cup	0
	COOKIES	
2	chocolate chip; 1 (2¼-inch diameter)	4
2	cream sandwich, chocolate; 1	4
1	sugar; 1 (2¼-inch diameter)	3
0	vanilla wafer; 1 (1⅜-inch diameter)	1
	CORN	
1	canned, cream-style; ½ cup	0
0	cooked; ½ cup	0
10	**CORN CHIPS;** 1 ounce	9
2	**CORNMEAL;** 1 cup	0
0	**CORNSTARCH;** 1 tablespoon	0
0	**CORN SYRUP;** 1 tablespoon	0

C (continued)

FAT (g)		CHOLESTEROL (mg)
2	**CRABMEAT,** cooked; 3 ounces	86
	CRACKERS	
1	butter, rectangular; 1	0
1	cheese, round; 1	1
1	graham; 2 squares	0
0	rye wafer, crisp; 2 (3½x1⅞ inches)	0
1	saltine; 2 (2-inch squares)	0
	CRANBERRIES	
0	cranberry juice cocktail; 1 cup	0
0	cranberry sauce; ½ cup	0
	CREAM	
5	light; 1 tablespoon	17
6	whipping; 1 tablespoon	20
0	**CUCUMBERS;** 6 large slices (1 ounce)	0

D—G

FAT (g)		CHOLESTEROL (mg)
0	**DATES,** fresh *or* dried, pitted; 10	0
	DOUGHNUTS	
8	cake-type, plain; 1 medium	25
11	yeast-type; 1 medium	11
	EGGS	
0	white; 1 large	0
6	whole; 1 large	253
5	yolk; 1 large	252
19	**EGGNOG;** 1 cup	149
0	**EGGPLANT,** cooked, chopped; ½ cup	0
8	**EGG SUBSTITUTE,** liquid; 1 cup	3
	FISH	
5	cod, broiled with butter; 3 ounces	69
0	flounder *or* sole, raw; 3 ounces	48
0	haddock, raw; 3 ounces	55
7	halibut, raw; 3 ounces	55
6	salmon, broiled with butter; 3 ounces	39
5	salmon, canned, pink; 3 ounces	30
9	sardines, canned, in oil, drained; 3 ounces	120
1	snapper, raw; 3 ounces	55
18	tuna, canned, in oil; 3 ounces	47
1	tuna, canned, in water; 3 ounces	54
1	walleye pike, raw; 3 ounces	48
	FLOUR, wheat	
1	all-purpose; 1 cup	0
2	whole wheat; 1 cup	0
12	**FRANKFURTER,** cooked; 1 medium	27
0	**GARLIC;** 1 clove	0
0	**GELATIN,** dry, unflavored; 1 envelope	0
30	**GOOSE,** cooked; 3 ounces	73
0	**GRAPEFRUIT,** fresh; ½ medium	0
0	**GRAPES,** green, fresh, seedless; ½ cup	0

91

FAT (g)		CHOLESTEROL (mg)
	H—O	
0	**HONEY;** 1 tablespoon	0
1	**HONEYDEW MELON;** ¼ medium	0
0	**HORSERADISH,** prepared; 1 tablespoon	0
0	**HOT PEPPER SAUCE;** 1 teaspoon	0
	ICE CREAM, vanilla	
7	ice milk; 1 cup	26
14	regular; 1 cup	53
14	soft-serve; 1 cup	53
0	**JAM;** 1 tablespoon	0
0	**KITCHEN BOUQUET;** 1 teaspoon	0
	LAMB	
6	leg roast, cooked, lean only; 3 ounces	85
6	loin chop, cooked, lean only; 3 ounces	84
9	rib chop, cooked, lean only; 3 ounces	86
13	**LARD;** 1 tablepsoon	12
0	**LEMON JUICE;** 1 tablespoon	0
0	**LENTILS,** cooked; ½ cup	0
0	**LETTUCE,** iceberg; ¼ medium head	0
1	**LOBSTER,** cooked; ½ cup	62
0	**MACARONI,** cooked; ½ cup	0
	MARGARINE	
12	regular; 1 tablespoon	0
5	spread, low calorie; 1 tablespoon	0
	MILK	
0	buttermilk; 1 cup	5
1	dried nonfat, instant, reconstituted; 1 cup	15
1	evaporated, skimmed, undiluted; 1 cup	8
20	evaporated, undiluted; 1 cup	78
5	low-fat (2%); 1 cup	22
0	skim; 1 cup	5
27	sweetened, condensed, undiluted; 1 cup	104
9	whole; 1 cup	34
	MUFFINS, baked from home recipes	
4	blueberry; 1	33
4	bran; 1	41
1	English; 1	2
4	plain; 1	21
0	**MUSHROOMS,** fresh, sliced; 1 cup	0
0	**MUSTARD,** prepared; 1 teaspoon	0
0	**NECTARINES,** fresh; 1 medium	0
1	**NONDAIRY TOPPING,** frozen; 1 tablespoon	0
1	**NOODLES,** cooked; ½ cup	25
	NUTS	
16	almonds, roasted; 1 ounce (about 22)	0
16	cashews, roasted; ¼ cup	0
18	peanuts, roasted; ¼ cup	0

FAT (g)		CHOLESTEROL (mg)
	H—O (continued)	
	NUTS (continued)	
21	pecans, chopped; ¼ cup	0
19	walnuts, chopped; ¼ cup	0
14	**OIL,** corn, olive, or soybean; 1 tablespoon	0
	OLIVES	
2	green; 4 medium	0
3	ripe; 4 medium	0
	ONIONS	
0	cooked, sliced; ½ cup	0
15	French-fried rings; 1 ounce	0
0	**ORANGES,** fresh; 1 medium	0
8	**OYSTERS,** raw; ½ cup (6 to 10 medium)	170
	P—S	
2	**PANCAKES,** made from mix; 1 (4-inch)	20
0	**PARSLEY,** snipped; 1 tablespoon	0
0	**PEACHES,** fresh; 1 medium	0
8	**PEANUT BUTTER;** 1 tablespoon	0
1	**PEARS,** fresh; 1 medium	0
0	**PEAS,** cooked; ½ cup	0
0	**PEPPERS,** green, sweet, chopped; ½ cup	0
0	**PICKLE RELISH,** sweet; 1 tablespoon	0
	PICKLES	
0	dill; 1 large (4x1¾ inches)	0
0	sweet; 1 medium (2¾x¾ inches)	0
	PIE; ⅛ of a 9-inch pie	
14	apple	0
11	lemon meringue	102
13	pumpkin	72
60	**PIE SHELL,** baked; one 9-inch	0
0	**PINEAPPLE,** fresh, chopped; ½ cup	0
0	**PLUMS,** fresh; 1 (2-inch diameter)	0
0	**POPCORN,** plain, popped; 1 cup	0
	PORK, cooked	
4	bacon, Canadian-style; 1 slice (1 ounce)	17
8	bacon, crisp strips, medium thickness; 2	13
13	chop, loin center cut, lean only; 3 ounces	74
19	ham, fully cooked, lean only; 3 ounces	77
8	picnic shoulder, fresh, lean only; 3 ounces	75
8	**POTATO CHIPS;** 10 medium	0
	POTATOES	
0	baked; 1 medium	0
4	french-fried, frozen, oven heated; 10 medium	0
1	sweet, baked; 1 medium	0

P—S (continued)

FAT (g)		CHOLESTEROL (mg)
0	PRETZELS; 10 small sticks	0
0	PRUNES, dried, uncooked, pitted; ½ cup	0
1	PUMPKIN, canned; 1 cup	0
0	RADISHES, raw; 5 medium	0
0	RAISINS; 1 cup	0
1	RASPBERRIES, fresh; ½ cup	0
0	RHUBARB, cooked, sweetened; ½ cup	0
	RICE	
1	brown, cooked; ½ cup	0
0	white, cooked; ½ cup	0
	ROLLS	
2	hamburger *or* frankfurter bun; 1	2
1	hard; 1 medium	1
10	sweet; 1 medium	27
	SALAD DRESSINGS	
1	blue cheese, low calorie; 1 tablespoon	0
8	blue cheese, regular; 1 tablespoon	3
1	French, low calorie; 1 tablespoon	0
6	French, regular; 1 tablespoon	0
1	Italian, low calorie; 1 tablespoon	0
9	Italian, regular; 1 tablespoon	0
11	mayonnaise; 1 tablespoon	10
2	mayonnaise-type, low calorie; 1 tablespoon	8
6	mayonnaise-type, regular; 1 tablespoon	8
2	Thousand Island, low calorie; 1 tablespoon	8
8	Thousand Island, regular; 1 tablespoon	8
0	SALT; 1 teaspoon	0
0	SAUERKRAUT, canned; ½ cup	0
	SAUSAGES AND LUNCHEON MEATS	
4	bologna; 1 slice	8
9	deviled ham; 1 ounce	18
7	Italian sausage; 1 ounce	21
12	pepperoni; 1 ounce	17
6	pork sausage, cooked; 1 link	12
1	SCALLOPS, cooked; 3 ounces	46
1	SHERBET, orange; ½ cup	0
13	SHORTENING; 1 tablespoon	0
	SHRIMP	
1	canned; 3 ounces	129
9	French-fried; 3 ounces	129
1	raw; 3 ounces	135
	SOUPS, condensed, canned, diluted with water unless specified otherwise	
0	beef bouillon, broth, *or* consommé; 1 cup	0
3	beef noodle; 1 cup	17

P—S (continued)

FAT (g)		CHOLESTEROL (mg)
	SOUPS *(continued)*	
0	chicken broth; 1 cup	0
2	chicken noodle; 1 cup	14
2	clam chowder, Manhattan-style; 1 cup	10
9	cream of celery, diluted with milk; 1 cup	25
14	cream of mushroom, diluted with milk; 1 cup	27
3	split pea soup; 1 cup	5
2	tomato; 1 cup	0
7	tomato, diluted with milk; 1 cup	18
2	vegetable with beef broth; 1 cup	10
48	SOUR CREAM, dairy; 1 cup	102
0	SOY SAUCE; 1 teaspoon	1
0	SPAGHETTI, cooked; ½ cup	0
0	SPINACH, fresh, torn; 1 cup	0
	SQUASH	
0	summer, cooked, chopped; ½ cup	0
0	winter, baked, mashed; ½ cup	0
1	STRAWBERRIES, fresh, whole; 1 cup	0
	SUGAR	
0	brown; 1 tablespoon	0
0	granulated; 1 tablespoon	0

T—Z

FAT (g)		CHOLESTEROL (mg)
8	TARTAR SAUCE; 1 tablespoon	0
5	TOFU (soybean curd); 4 ounces	0
	TOMATOES	
0	fresh; 1 medium	0
1	paste, canned; 6 ounces	0
0	sauce, canned; 8 ounces	0
	TORTILLAS	
1	corn; 1 (6-inch)	0
2	flour; 1 (6-inch)	0
14	TURKEY, roasted; 3 slices (3 ounces)	90
	VEAL	
11	cutlet, cooked; 3 ounces	86
12	loin chop, cooked; 3 ounces	76
0	VINEGAR; 1 tablespoon	0
5	WAFFLES; 1 section (4½x4½x⅝ inches)	63
0	WATER CHESTNUTS, canned and drained; 1 cup	0
1	WATERMELON; 1 wedge (8x4 inches)	0
13	WHIPPED TOPPING, mix; 1 envelope	0
	YOGURT	
1	fruit-flavored; ½ cup	5
2	plain; ½ cup	7

Index

Index

When it comes to health-conscious cooking, most of us need all the help we can get. That's why I'd like to suggest BETTER HOMES AND GARDENS® *Low-Salt Cooking* and *Low-Calorie Microwave Cook Book* as sensible sources of information for your better-health lifestyle.